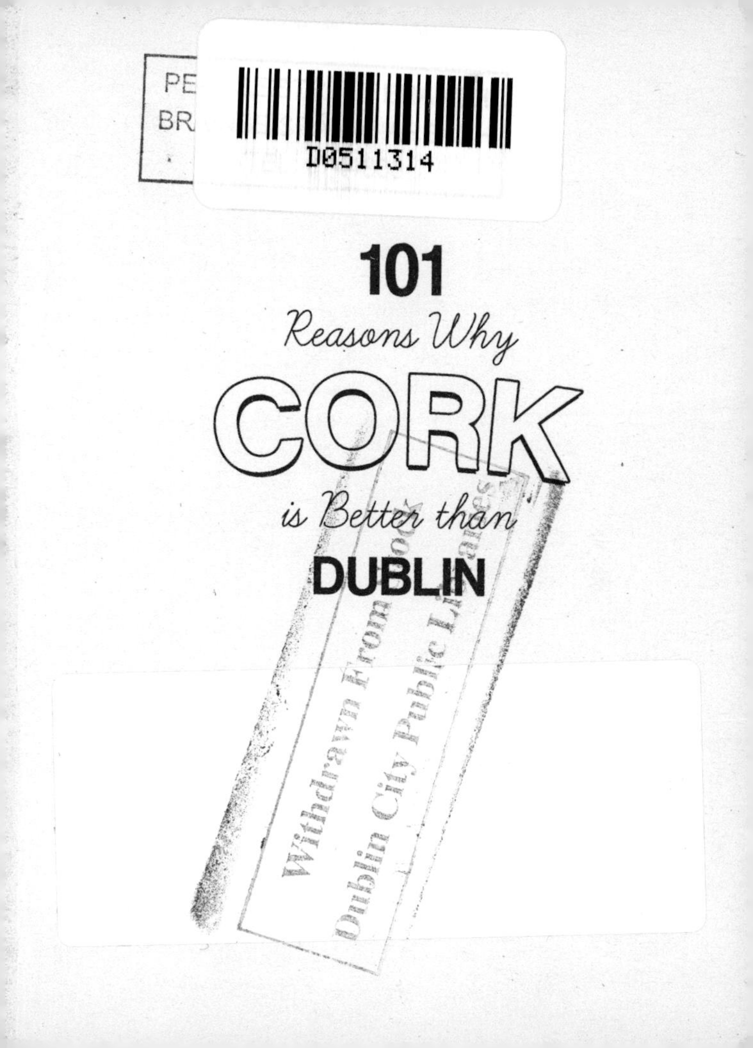

101 Reasons Why CORK is Better than DUBLIN

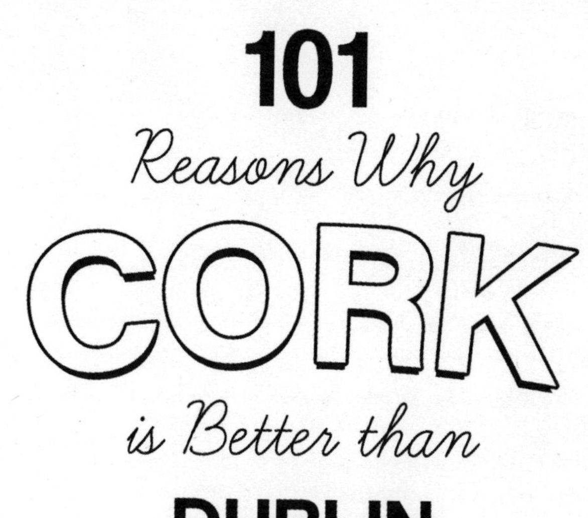

PAT FITZPATRICK

MERCIER PRESS

MERCIER PRESS
Cork
www.mercierpress.ie

ISBN: 978 1 78117 646 7

A CIP record for this title is available from the British Library

Printed and bound in the EU.

INTRODUCTION

Coming up with 101 ways that Cork beats Dublin isn't as easy as you might think.

First of all, whittling it down from 1,001 took the best part of a year.

Secondly, you have to juggle with the great conundrum – Cork has both a superiority and an inferiority complex when it comes to Dublin. We can be a bit funny that way.

Speaking of funny, Dublin readers should remember that most of what follows is supposed to be a joke. Also, don't forget to move your finger along under the words as you read and there's no shame in taking a guess at the bigger ones.

SECTION I

TOURIST ATTRACTIONS

1

THE ENGLISH MARKET

Four of the five most visited tourist attractions in the country are currently in Dublin. Top of the list is of course the Guinness Storehouse, where tourists can escape from the heroin addicts for a moment and enjoy an unobstructed view of Bargaintown on the other side of the Liffey. No wonder it's so popular.

The *Book of Kells* is a big draw in Trinity College. The book was stolen from the people of Meath and taken to Dublin, in the same way that the Parthenon Marbles were stolen from the Greeks by the Earl of Elgin and put on display in London. Acting like an English aristocrat is taboo in many parts of Ireland, but not so much in Trinity.

Of course none of these places can compare to the English Market in Cork. You can walk in for free and stare at Pat O'Connell, the fishmonger who has laughed at more royals than the guy who worked the guillotine during the French Revolution. Enjoy some authentic sights and smells, safe in the knowledge that you won't have to exit through a gift shop. And if food isn't really your thing, keep your eyes peeled for something you'll never see in a Dublin tourist attraction: locals. (Some say that's a plus when it comes to Dublin tourist attractions, but we'll stay nice.)

2
FITZGERALD PARK

Who cares that the Phoenix Park is the largest enclosed city park in Europe? It's a bit like boasting about the tallest mountain in Longford. The ideal city park is a quiet, central space where people from all over town can get together and eyeball each other. The Phoenix Park, on the other hand, is a giant field full of nervous deer, bad football and urban dogging. (You're never more than 400 metres away from a small crowd peering into a Kia Sportage.) Meanwhile, Dublin's smaller city parks like Stephen's Green and Merrion Square are for people who like listening to traffic.

Fitzgerald Park suffers from none of the above. Instead, it offers one of the great pleasures in life: looking across the Lee and wondering where Sunday's Well people get their money. And where else in the world would you get a Shakey Bridge that doesn't shake, a Hanging Garden that doesn't hang, and a museum with a photograph of Roy Keane?

Here's what you need to know about a decent park. Size doesn't matter. What you need is atmosphere, tranquillity, swans and the overwhelming smell of fake tan when families come in to take their Communion photos. Let's put it another way – you need Fitzgerald Park.

3

KINSALE

Some people reckon Kinsale is all about promiscuity. I can't comment because I'm from the town and still have relations living there, which could make it awkward the next time I meet them (at a swingers' party).

Sex aside, Dubliners reckon Kinsale isn't a patch on Dalkey or Howth, because their heads would explode with the notion that an off-DART town could be amazing. But the only area where Kinsale lags behind those two towns is in property prices (though there's not much in it, to be fair).

It boasts a drop-dead gorgeous harbour, the river, a couple of historic forts, and the Kinsale Rugby 7s event, which is popular with people who like drinking beer from a glass boot with a South Seas giant called Jasper. (Don't mock it until you've tried it!) That's before you sit down to have a drink in the sun outside The Bulman, or to eat at Fishy Fishy or The Black Pig or one of the other outstanding restaurants in town. Follow that with a guided walking tour and hear how much Irish (and American) history is stuffed into this one little town.

Dalkey and Howth can't compete. There's something for everyone in Kinsale – and no, that isn't a swingers' party reference, but I see where you're going and I like it.

4

THE BLARNEY STONE

Yanks. They bring out the worst in us. Of course you can't blame them for coming here in droves – after all, it's never a bad idea to put an ocean between yourself and Donald Trump. But all it takes is one sniff of a dollar and we're riverdancing like mad in front of them, trying to flog a CD of rebel songs and an authentic shillelagh fresh off the boat from Shanghai. If you doubt this, try to walk from Westmoreland Street through Temple Bar without passing a single begorrah. You can hardly blame the Dubs for cashing in, but it makes the centre of the capital feel like BallyMcPaddyLand.

If only Dublin had a castle in a nearby village

which would attract every visiting American within a radius of 100 kilometres, so they could pay to effectively snog every other American tourist that has ever visited the place, before popping into a large shop that sells quality Irish goods, so that when they come back into the city they are done with all the Paddy stuff.

That's Dublin's greatest tragedy – it doesn't have a Blarney Stone to suck the Paddy madness out of the Yanks, while also allowing us to keep our shillelagh flogging out of town.

5

DUBLIN DAY NIGHTMARE

9.30 a.m.: Lie on your bed, feeling sick, because you ate four breakfasts at the hotel buffet, having heard that Dublin can be expensive for lunch. It didn't help that you wolfed them down because the stag party at the next table was crying tears of vodka.

10.30 a.m.: Walk out of your hotel.

10.31 a.m.: Walk back into your hotel and google: 'Safe to go around Dublin on foot?'

10.35 a.m.: Get a taxi to the Guinness Store-house. Admire Bargaintown.

11.45 a.m.: Arrive in Temple Bar to immerse yourself in the local culture. Pay three separate buskers to stop murdering Ed Sheeran songs. (Those songs were dead already, lads.)

1.30 p.m.: Pub lunch. At least the three lads clod-hopping through Riverdance in the corner of the pub distract you from the spaghetti bolognese with Killarney sauce. (You asked for fusion cuisine, you got fusion cuisine.) You take a photo of your bill, because no one is going to believe the price.

4 p.m.: You stop for a pint in an iconic Dublin pub to sample the local culture. It is hosting a coachload of Chinese tourists, who are watching two alcoholics argue over the price of a pint of milk in 1992.

5 p.m.: You google '10 things to do in Dublin' and spot that 'Get the train to Cork' is number 2. (Cork people are relentless on the Internet.)

6 p.m.: You go to Cork.

6

CORK DAY DELIGHT

8 a.m.: Tell the guy serving you breakfast that you came down from Dublin. He looks sorry for you and says, 'I hear it's fierce busy.'

9 a.m.: Tell the woman at reception that you came down from Dublin. She looks sorry for you and says, 'I hear it's fierce busy.' You decide not to mention Dublin any more.

10 a.m.: Walk out of the hotel and down the South Mall. Most of the people seem happy to be alive; what's wrong with these people?

11 a.m.: You walk into the English Market. It isn't stall after stall of bearded hipsters pretending to be passionate about hand-crafted (insert latest trend here). That makes a change from

the Dublin markets you visited.

1 p.m.: Lunch costs less than twenty quid and doesn't come with Riverdance. Score.

3 p.m.: You pop into a local pub to sample some local atmosphere. This time it's a coachload of Japanese tourists watching two alcoholics arguing over who was the tall one in 'Cha and Miah'. (Not everything in Cork is different.)

5 p.m.: Someone smiles and says hello to you on Oliver Plunkett Street. They didn't seem like they were on drugs, but you can never be sure.

7 p.m.: You ask the Japanese waitress in the incredible Asian restaurant why Cork is so friendly. She asks if you were in Dublin. You say that you were. She says, 'I hear it's fierce busy.'

It is too.

7

KENT STATION

Pity the tourist who leaves the elegant red bricks and curvy platform of Kent Station, Cork, heading for Heuston Station in Dublin.

The best you can say for Heuston is that you no longer have to pay 20p to go to the jacks. The only thing we knew about that 20p fee was that it wasn't ring-fenced for toilet cleaning. The hygiene is still as you might expect – it's like Russian roulette trying to find a cubicle that won't remind you of the seventh circle of hell. (AKA, the pebble-dash puke Gouger managed to get out before he jumped on the 10.40 a.m. to Kildare.)

Still, this is more appetising than the onward journey into Dublin city centre. According to the map, the Luas Red Line crosses the Liffey outside Heuston and runs down Benburb Street. Most people from Cork feel they should have called it Head Back to the Joys of Kent Station and Cork Before It's Too Late Street – although they might have found it difficult to get that on a sign.

8

BUILDINGS, BY GEORGE

One of the great tragedies of Irish life is that half of Georgian Dublin was knocked down in the 1960s to make way for modern office blocks. The tragedy is that they didn't tear down the rest of Georgian Dublin while they were at it.

Open your eyes. Georgian Dublin is a po-faced, tight-lipped, buttoned-up kind of place. It's about as Irish as Rotterdam; it's about as exciting as a skiing holiday in Offaly. At the risk of sounding like Paddy MacProvo, it's also what you might call 'British'. According to some historians, the wide streets in Georgian Dublin were part of a broader initiative across Britain, after the French

Revolution, to make it easier for the cavalry to ride in and slaughter any pesky rebels. Yay Britain, well done for planning to kill us in our thousands!

Irish people grew up thinking that Georgian architecture was the envy of the world, a view that doesn't survive five minutes in Paris, Barcelona or Amsterdam. Or Cork, for that matter. Cork's architecture is chaotic and higgledy-piggledy. The nineteenth-century buildings that dominate the city centre are angular and pointy and slightly weird, a bit like the people who live there. They are like saucy poets compared to strait-laced Georgian Dublin, which brings to mind a sexually frustrated chartered accountant (as if there is any other kind).

9

PÁIRC UÍ CHAOIMH

There are two Croke Parks. The first one is where you sit in the lower tier and enjoy the match. The second is where you get a ticket in the upper tier and never once look at the pitch. It's a long way down, after all, and the balance wouldn't be great after the four pints you had for breakfast in Dublin city centre. (A bargain at €12. Each.)

You won't get vertigo in Páirc Uí Chaoimh. It's also a far nicer setting than Croke Park, unless you have a thing for kebabs and burnt-out cars. If you think the Munster Hurling Championship is competitive and cut-throat, wait until you see Ballintemple people showing off their wealth.

Some GAA people think it's a disgrace, the way Cork spent €110 million doing up the Páirc and now Dublin is going to have to pay for it. That's not the way it's viewed down on Leeside. For us, it's just nice to get back some of the money we've spent on fines over the years because we forgot to pay the shagging M50 toll. (Again.)

And hopefully part of the GAA's fund-raising campaign to pay for Páirc Uí Chaoimh will involve moving big matches out of Croke Park. We appreciate that none of these fixtures can include the Dubs, though, because they'll get a nosebleed if they pass Horse and Jockey. The poor boyz.

10

DE STATUES

It's true that Dublin has a lot more statues than Cork, even if it's mainly people standing still so they don't attract the attention of charity muggers, or 'chuggers', with clipboards who would like a quick word with you today. (The word is 'cash', in case you're wondering.)

Anyway, quantity doesn't mean quality. OK, the Oscar Wilde lounging-around one in Merrion Square is a lark – particularly when you look at his smug and superior face and realise why he's so popular in Dublin 4. But the other Dublin statues are just plain boring. The iconic one is Jim Larkin, with his arms out on O'Connell Street, shouting at the people below.

I think he's telling them he just got mugged, or even chugged.

Cork doesn't do statues, really, but when it does, at least they're a bit of laugh compared to Dublin's. The main statue in town is of teetotalist Father Mathew, pronounced Match-you. He tried to get Irish people to stop drinking. Come on, that's hilarious.

The other iconic statue is of the two guys looking up at the County Hall building, called 'Two Working Men'. (This represents the number of Cork people who had a job during the 1980s.) If you don't think that one of these guys is saying, 'Do you know, Mossie, that's taller than any building in Dublin?', then you know nothing about Cork.

11
GAOLS

I'm not talking about working prisons here. I doubt inmates in Cork prison reckon it's great to be locked up in the greatest city in the world. Unless they are actually from Cork, in which case I wouldn't rule it out.

But Cork is a clear winner when it comes to decommissioned prisons.

A sixth-century monastery and eighteenth-century military fortress before it became a prison that closed in 2004, Spike Island recently beat a host of iconic destinations when it was voted one of the leading tourist attractions in Europe. This came as news in Cork, given that ninety-nine per cent of us were unaware that Spike had become a tourist attraction, but we kept this to ourselves in case the judges changed their minds. Look, maybe 'witnessed a riot by imprisoned joyriders in the 1980s' was one of their criteria, so the poor Eiffel Tower never stood a chance.

Meanwhile, Cork city people have always had a soft spot for the Old Gaol, up towards Shanakiel. This is mainly because, back in the day, it gave a chance for poorer people to say their son was staying in Sunday's Well. (You're never more than two metres from a social climber in Cork.)

Sorry about that now Dublin, but you can keep your old Kilmainham. Cork is the ideal place if you love visiting the scene of other people's historic prison misery. (I'm sure the Germans have a word for it.)

12

HOLY HOUSES

Dublin has two cathedrals that date back to the Middle Ages: St Patrick's and Christ Church. It also has St Michan's, which houses the mummified remains of some of Dublin's most prominent families and dates back 400 years. (If you look closely, you can see their turned-up noses.)

At first glance, you'd say Cork couldn't compete. The oldest Catholic church in Cork is South Chapel, at 242 years of age (which is also the average age of the congregation). But who cares about age? The important thing is shelter. Face it, the only reason anyone visits a church when on holidays is because the snoozy locals have closed their shops for a siesta and you need somewhere to get in out of the heat. But this isn't an issue in Ireland. (At least not yet.)

And who wants to visit a church as a tourist, anyway? It's like the time Paul Gascoigne was asked by reporters why he didn't go to visit the Great Wall of China with his teammates. Gazza's reply? 'You've seen one wall, you've seen 'em all.'

It's the same with churches and cathedrals. You know the drill: walk in, whisper, light a few candles, stand next to a hot Italian and admire a portrait of the Annunciation with your serious, art-appreciation face, exit through the gift shop on your own.

If you really want a quick and quirky church visit when in Cork, then nothing can beat St Fin Barre's Cathedral on Leeside, home to the best golden angel in the world. Best of all, step outside and you're back in Cork. So thanks, but no thanks, Dublin, you can keep your auld churches.

13

CHRIST THE KING

New churches, now they're different. Christ the King is in Turners Cross, on the southside of Cork city. Travel books listed this as a must-see for visitors to Cork in the 1980s, because there wasn't much else going on. As a result, you'd see an exotic couple getting off the number 3 bus at Turners Cross and saying 'What the fuck?' to each other in Japanese.

OK, it's not quite Barcelona's Sagrada Família, but Christ the King is a grower. Designed by Chicago architect Barry Byrne, it looks like a jazz-age cinema crossed with a Mexican church in a spaghetti western. The arresting statue over the door depicts a Jesus with his hands outstretched, looking across towards the Turners Cross soccer ground, home of Cork City F.C., shouting, 'Jesus ref, that was never offside.' (Assuming he's the type to use his own name as a curse.)

Best of all, though, is the setting. Christ the King is a suburban art deco gem plonked down in between a pub, a chipper and the bookies. It's very Cork, and as surprising as a southsider who doesn't have delusions of grandeur. It's a must-see for visitors to Leeside; even better, there's no queue, and there's certainly nothing like it in Dublin.

14

BUTTER MUSEUM

The best thing about the name of Cork's most famous museum is that it doesn't include the word 'margarine'. But hang tough. First of all, it gets a four-star rating on TripAdvisor, and if you don't trust TripAdvisor, how come you keep using it to decide on a restaurant?

Some say nothing in this butter museum could possibly match the Ardagh Chalice in the National Museum of Ireland. I say, you can't put an eighth-century cup on your toast. Also, I would remind you of Gazza's views on the Great Wall of China, and add that once you've seen one priceless artefact, you've seen 'em all.

Anyway, if you really need to visit a big

museum, you can do far better than Dublin. (Let's face it, we've a poor record when it comes to colonising other countries, so you're stuck looking at stuff we stole from ourselves.)

Come on, you'll have a much better time in Cork's four-star Butter Museum than in anything Dublin has to offer. Plus, you'll learn something new and creamy and be back out on the streets of the best city in Ireland within the hour.

So spread the word. (Sorry.)

15

SHANDON BELLS

It's fair to say this is the best tourist attraction in the country.

First of all, there are no queues of Irish people forcing their English visitors to come and see it, just to prove we're not thick. (Hello, the *Book of Kells*.) Secondly, your initial reaction to Shandon is not, 'I thought it would be bigger.' (Hello again, the *Book of Kells*. Seriously, it's the size of a copybook.) Finally, a visit to Shandon won't expose you to Trinity students who wish they were Jacob Rees-Mogg. (I won't repeat myself.)

Shandon Tower takes you up above the city, where you can belt out 'Hey Jude' and the *Game of Thrones* theme tune on the bells for just a fiver.

The views are mixed, in fairness – unless you enjoy a nice multi-storey car park. But look, at least you can't see Bargaintown. (Hello again, the Guinness Storehouse.)

And on a clear day you can see all corners of Cork right down past Páirc Uí Chaoimh and the harbour. You can also catch the sounds of the city wafting up towards you, such as a local shouting, 'I'll give ye a tenner if ye promise not play "Hey Jude", the brain do be fried from listening to it.'

You see, you'd never get that in Dublin.

16

UCC

It's only right to pity people who went to UCD, and not just because they couldn't get in to Trinity. They paid good money for an education, only to find themselves the subjects in a cruel experiment, where young people are surrounded by horrible buildings for four years just to see how they react.

Some say they react by becoming a shower of intolerable tossers, but don't judge them until you've been through it yourself. Strange things happen when you spend too much time in a place that looks like the set of a movie called *Bow Down to Concrete, You Student Scum.*

Now, nobody is saying that UCC is perfect. There are far too many guys in Tipperary jerseys nicknamed after their home town; it's not unusual to find yourself at a history lecture next to a guy known to everybody as 'Clonmel'.

But when it comes to a soothing campus that isn't a detention centre for pompous bores (Hi again, Trinity), there is nothing to match the university on the Western Road in Cork. And before you ask, I'll deal with UCG in my next book, 573 Squillion Reasons Why Cork is Better than Galway. (And yes, I had to narrow that down too.)

17

DOUGLAS STREET

If you don't have time for a tour of all of Cork city, just go for a quick walk around Douglas Street. Nano Nagle Place is there, as well as the tower of the Red Abbey, an Augustinian friary founded in the thirteenth century. In 1690 the grounds of the abbey were used by Williamite forces under the Duke of Marlborough, who positioned cannons there to breach the city walls. It's OK to celebrate this now in a post-nationalist Ireland – unless the Brexit thing drags on for another fifty years and we all have to start hating the Brits again. (You'd be surprised how quickly it comes back.)

The other great historical site on Douglas Street is the iconic gay pub, Loafers. A safe haven for decades, Loafers is closed nowadays, probably because gay people are allowed to be themselves wherever and whenever they want. But the rainbow sign above the door serves as a reminder that we're not far removed from bigotry. (Alternatively, you could just turn on the international news.)

With that done, it's a choice between tapas in Iberian Way, live music in Coughlan's, or a pint in Fionnbarra's kooky beer garden. My advice is to try all three. And wonder if there is a street like this in Dublin while you're at it. (There isn't.)

18

THE VALUE

Hotel receptionist: 'No madam, that price just gets a room for the night; it doesn't actually buy you the hotel. Breakfast is €23 per person, and doesn't include toast or coffee or juice or anything really.'

The reason they call it a weekend break in Dublin is because, after the weekend, you're broke. €162.50 is the average cost of a hotel room in Dublin as I write. Anyone who pays that will probably end up in an average hotel room, on the wrong side of the M50. As you'd expect, the Germans have a word for it – *Raubritter*. This word comes from the robber barons on the Rhine who charged people extravagant tolls to pass through their stretch of the river. The same applies today, where the modern-day baron sits on the M50 and shouts, 'Hand over yizzers spondoolicks, yiz gullible bogtrotters, wha?'

You don't get this on Leeside. The best thing about a weekend break in Cork, as against Dublin, is going back home. Why? Because you still have a home to go to, seeing as you didn't have to sell it just to afford three days' parking in the capital.

19

PUBS 'N' CULTURE

You'll see them wandering around Dublin city centre, desperately looking for a hit, their dazed and dejected eyes crying out for something more to life than this. Welcome to a day in the life of a tourist walking around the capital, looking for local culture in the pubs.

The hit they want is a bit of real Ireland, anything to escape from this literary pub crawl hosted by an out-of-work actor dressed as Samuel Beckett. In fairness to him, the tour captures the spirit of Beckett – halfway through, everyone wonders if there is any point in carrying on.

Down the street, a Japanese family braces themselves before entering yet another Temple

Bar pub with demented diddily-aye Irish music leaking out the doors. Your Japanese isn't great, but it appears one of them is telling the others that he thought there would be more to Ireland than €8 pints and amateur Riverdance.

It turns out there is more to Ireland, and it's in Cork. The second city takes both music and drinking way too seriously to allow half the city centre to be turned into a theme park for Paddy Whackery. That's why there is a welcome shortage of diddily-aye. The only dodgy thing leaking out the door of a Cork pub is Donie, who has had a few and thinks he's in the jacks. I wouldn't recommend talking to him.

20

CALLANAN'S PUB

Dublin has a reputation for 'old man' pubs. They seem like a good place to visit, until one of the old men decides to talk to you. It turns out they all met Charlie Haughey at some point and put him straight on a few things. It also turns out that they wouldn't object if you bought them a pint.

There is no escape, it seems, until some bloke in a high-viz walks in and says: 'Drink up, we've run the numbers lads, this old man pub is no longer viable, and we need to turn it into a three-star hotel by tomorrow night.' This seems like a lucky escape, so you head for one of the newer pubs in Dublin city centre and squeeze in next to bride-to-be Kelli from Huddersfield, who has lost her hen party and is now drunk to the point of speaking Portuguese by accident. You phone your lawyer and ask if it's possible to sue Tourism Ireland under the Trade Descriptions Act.

Alternatively, you could just come to Cork and order a pint of Beamish in Callanan's on George's Quay. The pint is cheap, the snug is small, there's no TV, no music, no messing, no tapas; the only thing you can do is turn to the person next to you and start chatting. That doesn't just beat every pub in Dublin – it beats every pub, everywhere, ever.

21

'GOING JAZZING?'

Every year, towards the end of October, we stop using 'Hello, langer' as a greeting in Cork and say this to each other instead. It means 'Are you going to the jazz festival?'

This can mean different things to different people. Going jazzing means nodding along to a quartet if you are a genuine jazz aficionado in Cork – keep an eye out for all three of them in The Metropole Hotel.

After that, jazzing depends on your age. For people under forty it means drinking for fourteen hours and getting sick in a fountain while humming 'The Saints Go Marching In'. For people over forty, however, it means drinking for six hours, while still suffering a week-long hangover because you are getting old.

But more than anything, the festival brings people together. Say what you will about climate change, but the rain stayed away for the last few jazz festivals and Cork felt like New Orleans with Tanora. The buzz on the streets, whether at the *Día De Los Muertos* (Day of the Dead) opening parade or watching a free gig outside the Opera House, made it feel like something you'd never get in Dublin.

It was so good that it actually felt better than Galway, which is incredible, really, given that Galway is a 365-day street festival. (If you count a dreadlocked woman called Dreamzy playing bongos on Shop Street as a festival.)

22
DE HACKNEYS

Cork's cheap and convenient hackneys (cabs that can't be hailed on the street; instead, you have to phone for them or book online) aren't to everyone's liking. I got a tongue-lashing from a Dublin taxi driver once, just because I'm from Cork. 'Yizzers taxi drivers have totally surrendered to the hackney cabs below in Cork, yiz would never get away with that here in Dublin, know what I'm saying, wha?' said he in the I'm-your-friend-now-but-things-could-change voice that is preferred by drivers in the capital.

If you're actually the one paying for it, though, the Cork hackney experience is one of the great pleasures in life. There's something reassuring about pulling up outside your house bollocks drunk and the hackney driver saying, 'Is €8 all right?'

On top of that, the taxi shops I used on South Main Street at 2.30 a.m. on a Saturday morning were like the city in microcosm. One of the Frank and Walters sat next to me once and gave me half his salad burger. I'm devastated they didn't write a song about it: 'I said, try my salad burger it's niiice, he didn't need to be aaasked twiiiice.'

DE BUSES

I know they've got buses in Dublin too, but they're weak-ass ones that never had to go up a hill in their lives. What the capital is really missing, though, is Cork bus drivers, like the woman yesterday who refused to take the fare for my six-year-old daughter because, 'Ah sure, ye're on yeer way home, like.' Maybe that's official Bus Éireann policy, you can never tell.

The Irish habit of bus driver thanking goes a step further in Cork, where disembarking passengers pretty much feel like offering them a sex act. (They have just saved us walking up a hill in the rain, so there's no shortage of goodwill.)

Top tip for visitors: most Cork bus routes run

though the city centre, south to north. You'll know the bus is getting close to the river when the posh types start edging towards the exit, terrified they'll miss their stop and end up on the northside. ('A lot of them never even played tennis, Monica.')

Second top tip for visitors: there is every chance the person sitting next to you on the bus will strike up a conversation. Don't worry if you can't understand them, the truth is we talk funny. Just nod every thirty seconds and let Jerry tell you about his eldest fella out in Perth.

24

THE NINETY-MINUTE RULE

Drive ninety minutes in any direction from Dublin and you'll still find yourself in close proximity to a man by the name of Whiplash, a friendly aggressive Dubliner who is dying to talk about a fight he had in Skerries once, although he calls it 'a digging match'.

You won't find Whiplash in Cork because he comes out in spots if he goes south of Urlingford. It's his loss, though, given the options you'll find within ninety minutes from Cork city.

Leave Cork city at 10.30 a.m. and you'll be staring out at Bantry Bay by noon. There are other places you can reach from Cork in that time too, including Waterford and Limerick. (If you are stuck. Really stuck now, like.)

Leave Dublin city at 10.30 a.m. and by noon you are on the M50. At 1 p.m., you are still on the M50. 2 p.m.: M50. If you'd left from Cork, you could be digging into a plate of mussels near Glandore round about now. But you chose to leave from Dublin, so you're still on the M50. You might get to Mullingar by 3 p.m., if you're lucky. (In which case, we might want to change your definition of lucky. Nothing against Mullingar, but you know yourself.)

25
CORK AIRPORT

The good news is that Dublin Airport is one of the fastest growing airports in Europe. The bad news is that the last time this happened the economy tanked and the country ended up with €43.40 in the bank. So now might be a good time to sell your house.

If you feel like booking a flight with the money, then I'd suggest flying from Cork.

Unlike Dublin Airport, the long-term car park is not actually located in Kildare. The drive there doesn't involve the M50, or a cab ride where the bleedin' taxi driver makes you glad you're leaving the country.

True to the noble Cork tradition of spending

a fortune on white elephants, our airport is about twice the size it needs to be, so it never feels packed. It's not too big either, though. Unlike Dublin, there won't be an army of volunteers handing out energy drinks and foil blankets at your gate because you just completed a 10k run from security.

Likewise, when you arrive into Cork, it doesn't feel like your plane landed 15 kilometres from the terminal and they forced you to walk the last bit, surrounded by ads for Bunratty Castle. Instead, a mere fifteen minutes after you land, you're in a taxi on the way into town, listening to the driver telling you why he'd hate to live in Dublin. And who could blame him?

26

THE JACK LYNCH TUNNEL

The original and best tunnel in Ireland is about to get even better.

If politicians are to be believed (geddit?) traffic congestion around the Jack Lynch will come to an end shortly, with a series of swanky flyovers replacing the Dunkettle Roundabout.

Talk about an impending disaster for national radio stations – they'll have to come up with something other than 'The usual tailbacks at the Dunkettle Roundabout' as the sum total of their traffic report from Cork.

(Top tip: you can always spot the rush-hour drivers in Cork listening to a traffic report on a national station – they're the ones screaming at the radio.)

The best traffic news for Cork is that the new and improved Jack Lynch Tunnel is expected to stay free of charge. This is in contrast to the €1.90 it currently costs to avoid Limerick (which would be cheap at twice the price, says you).

Meanwhile, the Dublin Port Tunnel charges €10 at peak time for those driving a car. Maybe they could reduce the price by selling the naming rights of the tunnel to some corporate interest. Better still, change the name to something more appropriate, like: 'The One Final Bit of Gouging Before Yiz Head Home to Yizzers Bog Houses Tunnel'. Just because it's a mouthful doesn't make it wrong.

27

PATRICK'S STREET

O'Connell Street, sure where would you be going? Anywhere else and in a hurry, says you. Our national main street could do with a rebranding, seeing as it's about as popular with Irish people as cleaning up after yourself on the beach. (We wouldn't be great at that.)

The first step in rebranding O'Connell Street would be to change the name. 'Fight or Flight Street' would capture it nicely – or maybe go all-in on the reality front and just call it 'Poundland'.

Patrick's Street is different, and not just because it has a dopey nickname. It's known locally as 'Pana', a four-letter word that takes ten seconds to say because Cork people like to stretch out their As. Paaana isn't much better than O'Connell Street when it comes to shops, but where it does win is as a main stage of sorts for the city, where the people can promenade up and down, eyeballing each other.

It's also where we gather to re-enact one of the great rituals of Cork life. That is where you shout, 'You're looking well, Gerry boy, did you lose a bit of weight?' at someone and then wait until they're out of earshot before muttering, 'I can't go out the door without bumping into that fat langer.' That's Cork for you in a nutshell.

28

WALK THIS WAY

When Paaana was closed to traffic every afternoon in 2018, some fools thought it was the first step towards complete pedestrianisation. This is crazy – Paaana has been a pedestrian street for as long as anyone can remember. So has every other street in town. Waiting for a green man to cross the road in Cork marks you out as either a loser or a visitor from Dublin. (Insert your own joke here.)

Here is what you need to know, as a tourist. Say you are walking down Paaana and spot someone you know coming out of Penney's on the other side of the street – the proper response here is to walk straight across the road with your hand in the air, saying 'sorry, sorry, sorry' at any motorists in the vicinity. Anyone who blows their horn doesn't know the way things go in Cork, and they are probably just down for the day from Kanturk.

Blowing your horn at a pedestrian in Cork is actually worse than knocking down a cow in India, because at least over there you don't have a crowd of people shouting, 'Keep your horn for your wife, you langer, he's only trying to cross the road to say hello to his friend.'

Before we leave our section on jaywalking, let's just say that they aren't as kind to pedestrians in Dublin. (How ya doing, Dame Street?)

29

THE RIVER LEE

The Liffey is a second-rate river. In the unlikely event that somebody wrote an ode, it would start: 'Oh Liffey, oh Liffey, your smell's a bit iffy; I turned my back on my bike, it was gone in a jiffy'.

For starters, it doesn't even rise in County Dublin; I mean, that's just plain embarrassing. Cork people would hate to come from a county that was so small it couldn't even contain the source and estuary of a decent river. Then there's the fact that the Liffey's weak dribble isn't strong enough for a dam, so Cork, Limerick and assorted bogmen have to generate the electricity for the LUAS. Outrageous.

Contrast that with the lovely Lee, splitting

into two channels by the County Hall to reunite later down by the Idle Hour, making an island of the city centre and allowing Cork people to call their hometown 'the Venice of the North'. It's a compelling case, for anyone who has never been to Venice.

As you might have heard, the Lee flows into the second-deepest natural harbour in the world, which has long been a source of pride to Cork people, since someone pointed it out to us last week. (Harbour size suddenly went from 'who cares' to 'must have' down on Leeside. We'll take our wins where we can find them.)

SECTION 2

THE LOCALS

30

FRIENDLINESS

Cork was voted the third friendliest city in the world in 2018. This came as a complete surprise, because it meant that there were two cities in the world friendlier than Cork. (We pride ourselves on being super-friendly to outsiders, while also believing that there is no one better than one of our own. Go figure.)

Our other problem with the survey was that Dublin was voted the seventh friendliest city on earth, only four places behind Cork. It completely undermined our faith in this random poll that we'd never heard of until it appeared in the *Examiner*. How could we possibly trust anyone who visited Dublin and managed to miss that it's the least friendly place on earth, not to mention fierce busy? But ultimately this was something on the Internet that said we were better than Dublin, so you'd be a fool to ignore it.

There is of course one reason Cork will always appear friendlier than Dublin, and that's the accent. It's hard not to warm to someone when they are basically singing at you like a cockatoo. Meanwhile, the nicest person in Dublin can't help sounding like they are going to nick your car. (And that's just the posh ones.)

31

PACK OF FLAS

Don't ask me about the spelling. It could be flas, flaas, flahs, or flase, as in vase. It definitely isn't fleadhs. Nobody looks good playing the squeeze box.

Flas is the collective noun in Cork for a pack of good-looking people. It derives from the verb, to fla, which is to engage in sexual intercourse with someone, or defraud them, or both. It is streets ahead of the Dublin term, 'bleedin' ride', which sounds very painful.

So Dublin or Cork: where will you find the bigger pack of flas? Don't expect to find your answer on the Internet. Put 'Good Looking Cork or Dublin' into Google and that's an afternoon wasted looking at photos of horny men and women in your area. It could be worse, I suppose, but it proves nothing.

Deep down though, when it comes to flas, we all know Dublin has no one to compete with the likes of Hilary Rose, Sarah Greene, Roy Keane, Peter O'Mahony, Cillian Murphy and Jonathan Rhys-Meyers. And if they do, I wouldn't mind meeting them, says you.

Also, emergency departments in Dublin don't have to deal with Saturday Night Whiplash. This is where visitors out on the town in Cork hurt themselves by turning around too quickly to look at a looker. Ask anyone, they've fierce problems with that in Cork University Hospital. Like I said, we're a pack of flas.

32

SENSE OF HUMOUR

If there were Internet dating for cities, Dublin's profile would mention its two intersecting tram-lines and world-famous sense of humour. This would come as news to anyone who ever asked a Dublin taxi driver if he had change of €50. 'I do in me bollix,' says he, laughing at his own joke in a way that suggests he's going to drop you by the side of the road in Mulhuddart. The truth? Dublin is more GOSH than GSOH.

Cork people are just funnier. Some people find this hard to believe because Cork doesn't have many stand-up comedians; these people have obviously never spent five minutes talking to a stand-up comedian.

Cork's sense of humour is built for purpose, which is to undermine anyone who ever tries to achieve anything and remind them that they're still just a langer. For example, Peter Stringer got accolades from all over the world when he announced his retirement from rugby; when he went into his local gym in Cork the following day, however, the guy at the desk asked, 'Do you have a job yet?' In other words, never forget, you're just a langer like the rest of us.

It's the kind of thing you can say to any Cork person who has tasted success. Except Roy Keane. Don't try it on Roy Keane. Seriously, don't.

33

THE MEANING OF LANGER

As the great Billy Connolly pointed out, the term 'fuck off' is completely unambiguous. Billy correctly spotted that you never hear the phrase 'Fuck off, he hinted.'

Langer is the opposite – it can mean anything you want, particularly in the hands of a Cork person. (No need to send a letter to the Office for Public Decency, complaining that I'm talking about Cork people with langers in their hands. It's not my fault that you have a filthy mind.)

The meaning of langer is all in the length of the letter L. The long L (You're some lllllllllll-ang-er) means trouble. Basically, if you go the toilet as the langer word starts, and the other person is still on the L when you get back, it might be a good idea to leave.

On the other hand, if it's the short L, you could be looking at marriage. 'Do you take this langer to be your lawfully wedded husband?' 'I do. Give us a kiss, ya complete fla, ya.'

(A word in your ear, Bernhard, before I go. You might think it's funny for a leading German golfer to openly admit that he's a langer. But a generation of Cork golf fans are still in therapy with the shock.)

34

SELF AWARENESS

No one in Cork would deny that Dublin is the capital city. Of delusion. As I write, it's suffering from the notion that it's going to become the new London after Brexit. Because nothing says 'high-flying metropolis' faster than a posse of bankers riding into town and pushing up property prices so that everyone else has to go live in Swords.

At the heart of Dublin's delusion is the LUAS. Dubliners are so happy that their two tramlines finally intersect that they don't seem to have noticed that the fastest traffic route from the northside to the southside is now via Holyhead.

The notion that two-line LUAS Dublin is a player on the world stage lasts until you visit

Berlin, where you can pretty much get a tram to the jacks. Then you go on to Nearbystadt, which is the size of Mallow, and it turns out you can get a tram to the jacks there as well.

Cork has none of these delusions. The whole 'Real Republic' thing is just a ruse to sell T-shirts to tourists. The fact is that Cork knows its place in the world. (Which, just to be clear, is ahead of Dublin, Limerick, Galway, Waterford and Sligo.)

35

CLIMATE RAGE

Corcaigh, which is the Irish for 'Cork', is also the Irish for 'marsh', so it's not like we're trying to hide the fact that it can be a bit damp. The statistics suggest that Cork is sopping, with an annual average rainfall of 1,050 millimetres, compared to Dublin's 738 millimetres.

It's not as bad as it seems, however. 1,000 of those 1,050 millimetres typically fall during the October Bank Holiday weekend, when most of Cork is locked (and I mean locked) indoors pretending to like jazz. Or at least a band from Swansea playing 'Living Next Door to Alice'.

The other thing is, we love when it rains in Cork. Why? Because it allows us to experience

De Outrage. Here's how De Outrage works:

Radio host on national broadcaster says: 'Lovely morning here in Dublin, hope it's nice wherever you are.'

Listener in Cork looks out the window. It isn't nice where she is; in fact, it's pissing down Gangnam style. Listener in Cork is overcome with rage because that gowl in Dublin couldn't be bothered to check the nationwide weather forecast. This feels fantastic, because as Donald Trump could tell you, nothing feels better than a bit of rage.

You see, every cloud …

36
DRUG FUN

It isn't just about scenery. Cork has always prided itself on being a centre for world-class pharmaceuticals – just ask anyone who went to Sir Henry's nightclub in the 1990s. But these days it's the legitimate side of the drug trade that has turned Leeside into a hub for multi-national pharmaceuticals. GlaxoSmithKline, Johnson & Johnson, Novartis and others have large manufacturing and research facilities located in the greater Cork area.

Pfizer are the real heroes, however, with their decision to locate Viagra production at their plant in Ringaskiddy. The blue pill has made a massive contribution to growth in Ireland, says you, always on the lookout for a cheap laugh. Speaking of cheap laughs, local wags claim the Ringaskiddy area is a perfect base for clinical trials, because Carrigaline is full of langers. (Don't blame me for local wags, I just write what they say.) But it's good to see, at least, that Cork can mix comedy and world-class manufacturing plants.

Contrast this with po-faced Dublin, where the main industry involves filling offices with beanbags and table-tennis tables for social media companies that will likely be gone in five years. There's no sense to that.

37

CORK MODESTY

Cork people aren't as brash as you might think. Just look at the top three counties, in ascending order of cockiness.

3: Cork Modesty. We live in the best city in Ireland, don't we, seriously, ah, come on, please, I know we're always on about Tanora and Roy Keane, but this superiority thing is actually a cover for our giant inferiority complex, particularly after we went to New York and realised that the Lough is no match for Central Park, do you know that kind of a way? And like, it's great that we keep getting voted as the best city in the world in some poll or whatever, but deep down we know the poll has probably been skewed by our cousin Paul, who did a PhD in Voting Robots in CIT. I suppose this is just an awkward way of saying we're not that sure of ourselves.

2: Dublin Modesty. Bono.

1: Kerry Modesty. Yerra, we're not the worst.

SECTION 3

FAMOUS PEOPLE

38

ROY KEANE

You can stop reading now if you are tight for time. We lead busy lives these days, after all, and there must be something better you could be doing with your time than ploughing all the way through 101 great Cork things that I stole from a discussion on Reddit. (Only messing, at least half of them were nicked from boards.ie.)

You see, the truth is that Cork will always beat Dublin, because it gave the world Roy Keane.

Bono is the most famous living Dublin person, and the only way he could top Roy is in a song contest. (This probably isn't true, but as we say in Cork, it's nice to be nice.)

Roy is so cool, the best thing Dublin people

can do in response is to form a queue to ghost-write his latest autobiography (how're ya, Eamon Dunphy and Roddy Doyle).

Here is a man who walked away from the Irish camp in Saipan in 2002, so we could fool ourselves into thinking that, if he'd stayed, we could have won the World Cup. He never gets enough credit for that.

Roy Keane also inspired a song by Morrissey ('Roy's Keen'), back when Morrissey was cool. Morrissey could have chosen to write a song about his distant relative, Dublin's Robbie Keane (who knew!), but he didn't. He chose Roy.

39

ELIZA LYNCH

I'm not saying the capital doesn't produce famous women. It's just that Dublin never gave the world a woman who went on to become the unofficial queen of Paraguay. (Or official, for that matter – it's not like Paraguay was ever ruled by a Queen Howyiz.)

If Eliza Lynch had been from Dublin, there'd probably be a LUAS line named after her.

But she was from Charleville in County Cork, so you've probably never heard of her, and neither had I until I started researching this book. She was born there in 1833 and moved to France with her family, where she was tricked into marrying a French army officer at the age of sixteen. (And you thought you lived a crazy life because you smoked half a joint when you went to Cape Cod on a J1.)

Eliza fled and ended up marrying a billionaire who later became president of Paraguay. Score! Despised by the local elite, she was popular with the common people and entertained them with parties that went on for months. Anyone who reckons this is an exaggeration has never been to a wedding in Charleville. She died in Paris in 1886. Fair play.

40

JACK LYNCH

Brian Boru got a bridge across the Lee named after him, without ever once captaining Cork or saving the country from a potential civil war in the early 1970s. So a mere bridge was never going to be enough for Jack Lynch, which is why we named the tunnel after him. (I remember a council official at the time outlining the two reasons why they went for a tunnel under the Lee. 1: A tunnel is the most expensive option. 2: Dublin doesn't have one. If this story isn't true, it should be.)

The Dublin taoisigh are no match for Jack. You couldn't name a tunnel after Bertie Ahern, because the Internet would break with all the jokes about dig-outs. The only thing Bertie managed to get named after him, the Bertie Bowl, didn't even get built.

I won't pull a cheap shot and claim that Charlie Haughey was from Dublin. As he pointed out himself, he was actually born in Castlebar, and whatever else you might think about Charlie, he was always a man who liked to tell the truth.

The only taoiseach who can compare to Jack is Leo Varadkar. Like Jack, he is doing everything in his power to help his native county win six consecutive All-Ireland football championships, by diverting ninety per cent of the national tax revenue to Dublin GAA. Seriously Dubs, give that man a tunnel!

41

CILLIAN MURPHY

The Wind That Shakes the Barley, *Batman Begins*, *Inception*, *28 Days Later*, I don't need to go on. But it's his Thomas Shelby in *Peaky Blinders* that has everyone talking. Some say they can't believe how convincing he is playing the part of a Birmingham gangster. I say they needed an actor to play a cranky guy from a second city with a funny sing-song accent and a chip on both shoulders – like, that is a step-by-step guide to building your own Cork man.

Maybe if he appeared on Graham Norton once a month with a brand new nose, we'd appreciate Cillian Murphy for the A-list actor that he actually is. But he refuses to play the fame game, preferring DJing at the Skibbereen Arts Festival to making a clown of himself on a couch.

Colin Farrell or Brendan Gleeson & Sons just can't match that kind of cool. People who know Murphy say he is also incredibly sound, which is devastating for those of us secretly hoping he'd be a langer so we needn't feel so bad about ourselves.

Cillian Murphy even makes the odd mistake, just to show he's human. The main one is, of course, moving from London to Dublin a couple of years back, when he could have chosen Cork. This came as a crushing blow on Leeside and, to be honest, we're still trying to pretend it didn't happen.

42

EILEEN WALSH

This legend of a Cork actress has shown her serious side in *Eden* and *The Magdalene Sisters*. She also made us laugh in *Pure Mule*, which is quite an achievement, because there's nothing funny about a Midlands accent. But it's her more recent appearances in *Catastrophe* that really caught the eye. It was confusing for Cork people to watch the Channel 4 show at first, because Sharon Horgan is amazing in it, even though she's only from Meath. (The grudge from the 1988 All-Ireland football final do be alive and well and living all over Cork.)

Eileen Walsh stars as the friend over on a visit from Ireland to London. Her hilarious character,

Kate, pretty much doubled the number of visitors to Leeside – they nearly had to lay on extra planes as people flew in to see if everyone in Cork likes to take ecstasy and leave their husband to go live with some randomer on a boat. (That does sound very Blackrock Road, now that you mention it.)

As if that wasn't enough, Eileen then popped up on Sky's hit *Patrick Melrose*, and made Benedict Cumberbatch look average. Beat that, you Dublin actors.

43

SIOBHÁN McSWEENEY

Cork is Funnier than Dublin 2 – This Time She's a Nun.

At the time of writing, the two best things on Irish TV have nothing to do with Dublin. *Derry Girls* and *Young Offenders* have broken big in the UK, even though neither of them comes with subtitles.

We don't want to muscle in on Derry's moment – they seem like very nice people when they travel down here twice a year to lose to Cork City. But there's no escaping the fact that the funniest thing on *Derry Girls* is the head nun at the school, and she's played by Siobhán McSweeney, who is indeed from Cork.

Siobhán is hardly a newcomer, with roles in *The Wind That Shakes the Barley*, *The Fall*, *Collateral* and other top-notch shows. She was also on *Emmerdale* once as a nurse, but sure look we all make mistakes.

Her theatre performances have been a big hit with members of the Cork intelligentsia – both of them went to see her in *Autumn Royal* recently at The Everyman. This was written by honorary Corkman, Kevin Barry. Kevin is from Limerick. As embarrassing as this must be for him, it's even worse for native Cork writers, because he captures life on Leeside better than the lot of us put together. (Langer.)

44

BILL AND GRAHAM

Everybody loved the late Bill O'Herlihy, and not just because he could squeeze seven syllables into the word 'live'. Here in Cork, he remains as popular as starting every second sentence with 'to be honest with you'. (Sidebar – this is a clear tell that we are lying.)

Bill wasn't just entertaining, he was a consummate professional, with the way he fired soccer questions at Eamon Dunphy, Johnny Giles and Liam Brady on TV during every major Irish soccer occasion from the 1980s all the way up to the 2000s. Seriously, it couldn't have been easy for a Cork man to make a career out of pretending to know less than three guys from Dublin.

It's a shame he never got a shot at hosting a chat show. I won't hear a word against Gay Byrne, Pat Kenny or Ryan Tubridy, because I'm waiting for Tubridy to invite me on *The Late Late Show* to plug this book. (Hi, Ryan!) But they are all from Dublin and it might be time to spread the love and give the gig to someone from Cork.

Graham Norton is probably too busy, what with him basically owning the chat show game in London. Just like Bill, he's proof that your Dublin types will never match Cork for the anchorman banter.

45

MATT AND BRENDAN

Speaking of anchorman banter, what about Matt Cooper and Brendan O'Connor? You couldn't question their judgement, even though they both chose to leave Cork and live in Dublin.

Matt probably couldn't fit in *The Late Late*, what with him having seventy-four other jobs.

As for Brendan, I should point out that I know him, but this doesn't make me biased, because Cork people are brutal to their friends. That said, he would be a perfect fit for *The Late Late*. Say what you will about the previous Dublin hosts, but not one of them wrote and performed a novelty rap record that spent fifteen weeks in the Irish charts, peaking at number three, like our

Brendan. Ask any Irish person over thirty who's in the house, and they know the answer is Jesus. The Catholic Church would struggle to get that kind of name recognition for their main man.

Like Matt, Brendan has about fifty-four jobs in the media. The two are a testament to the Cork work ethic. Kids in other counties are told to head up to Dublin and get themselves a job. Kids in Cork are told to head up to Dublin and get themselves all the jobs, so there will be none left for the Dubs. (This is in fact true.)

46

DENIS O'CONNOR

He is probably known as Denis Who? by now, because people have short memories. But put 'Denis O'Connor sawn-off shotgun Glanmire 2018' into Google and you'll see where I'm going. Denis was the eighty-three-year-old who wasn't one bit happy when three hooded youths broke into his favourite bookmakers with hammers and a sawn-off shotgun. So he gave one of them a shove and joined forces with the manager to run them off the premises. The same punter in Dublin would probably have pocket-dialled *Liveline*.

But Denis is from cranky Cork. Maybe it's the humidity down here, or the shocking number of midges around during the summer months, but people on Leeside aren't keen on being pushed around. Roy Keane, Ronan O'Gara, Sonia O'Sullivan, even super nice guys like Peter Stringer have a special pissed-off look you don't find elsewhere. It's the same look Denis used on the armed thugs as he roared 'cowards' and showed them the door.

47

THE O'DONOVANS

Gary and Paul O'Donovan have turned rowing into the most nerve-racking sport in the world. All of Ireland is on edge when they're competing, terrified we'll get our timings wrong and miss the post-race interview with the two lads. (Come on, it's not like we're tuning in to watch the rowing. As spectator sports go, it's up there with watching paint dry, while on Valium, in Urlingford. As they pointed out themselves, it's simply into the water and pull like a dog.)

The TV interviews get funnier the more you watch them, just like Road Runner cartoons. For example, when Graham Norton asked if it was hard to get back into the water after the buzz of the Olympics, Paul said, no, they just lowered the boat down and sat in. Funny.

A documentary on YouTube – The Rowing Brothers Who Shocked the World – is worth a look and not just because of the way West Cork people pronounce Doh-limpicks. The documentary charts the story of Skibbereen Rowing Club, a community affair run on goodwill and sandwiches, where they make the weights for their gym from some locally scrounged scrap metal. I'm not going to compare this with Dublin GAA and Leinster rugby, because I don't want to keep banging on about buying success. But you know what I mean.

48
SEÁN MURRAY

Staying in Skibbereen, let's talk about bra opening. (Stop pretending you were expecting me to say that.)

In the video about the O'Donovans, there is a vignette for local clothes-shop owner Seán Murray, who holds the world record for the number of bras opened in a minute. It's ninety-one. If you think you can do better, bear in mind that he does it one-handed. (This is in keeping with the old rural tradition in Ireland, where a man is expected to know how to open his wife's bra without putting down his pint.)

There is an eye-catching moment in the video, as Seán works his way along the line of women's backs, doing his thing. The eye-catching bit is that they aren't all women. A bunch of them at the end are men, or 'min' as they'd be known locally. You can see the determination in their eyes. Another man might have smirked if he found himself standing in a West Cork clothes shop, while the owner relieved him of his bra. But all these locals wanted was for Seán to break the world record. Because if Seán Murray can open more bras than anyone in the world that means he can open more bras than anyone in Dublin. And that's all that matters.

49

JOHN CREEDON

John Creedon is the least cool guy in the world. He is also the most cool guy in the world.

He first popped up as Terence in 'Tell it to Terence', a camp Cork hairdresser-cum-agony-aunt who appeared on Gerry Ryan's RTÉ radio show during the 1980s. Let's just say you wouldn't hear that sort of thing on the radio today, and not just because Gerry is no longer with us.

But listen to a couple of clips on YouTube and try not to laugh. You might even cry a little, as there's plenty of pathos in his take on a character that goes way beyond a two-dimensional camp hairdresser.

Today, most people know Creedon from his

radio show on RTÉ Radio 1. It's like a hug for people who love good music. You're on a long drive on a Monday night, trying to avoid the latest hits, classic hits, hits and memories, all-time latest classic hits, when you stumble on Creedon's show, from RTÉ in Cork. He's playing a song by a guy called something like Smokin' Bob Michigan, who once shared a bus with Neil Young. You like the sound of Smokin' Bob and wish you'd heard of him before. The song over, Creedon says hello to Mike and Jane, who are in a caravan in Lahinch. You drive on, thinking that everything is going to be OK with the world. Let's just say you wouldn't get that from *Liveline*.

50

JIMMY CROWLEY

And you thought Beyoncé was a survivor. Jimmy Crowley started playing folk music before they invented it – he's so unique he doesn't even have a beard. He's the senior figure in the Cork singer-songwriter tradition that includes the likes of Mick Flannery and John Spillane. As well as that, he's also the main curator of local folklore and songs.

Crowley's speciality is Cork songs, which just don't sound right in another accent. And yes I am talking about the Wolfe Tones singing 'The Boys of Fairhill'. And yes, it doesn't stop there.

Listen to Jimmy singing the famous folk song 'Salonika', then listen to The Dubliners' version and you'll appreciate that some things are better in a Cork accent. Basically, hands off our songs, ye beardy Dubs.

But Crowley's finest moment is undoubtedly 'The Pool Song'. Written by Con Ó Drisceoil from down around Skibbereen, it is a lament for the way music was driven out of pubs by pool tables. Crowley dials the Cork up to 11 in a genius of a song that manages to take the piss out of the past and present at the same time. You won't be surprised to hear that The Dubliners sang their own version of it. Jesus, you'd swear they had no songs of their own.

51

MICHAEL COLLINS

The good news is that Michael Collins was from Cork. The bad news is the guy who reportedly killed him was also from Cork. (I could have had a field day if he was from Dublin. Still, you can't have everything.)

Collins had more about him than merely plotting the downfall of the British Empire. The Big Fella was a hit with the women too, which suggests his nickname wasn't just a reference to his height, says you.

Mr Lova Lova, as he isn't known, is mourned as the man who could have saved Ireland from forty years of de Valera, if only he hadn't died young. All I know is he'd probably have moved the capital to Cork and we'd have been stuck with nothing to bitch about. So maybe the guy who shot him did us all a favour!

That man is widely believed to be Denis 'Sonny' O'Neill. He didn't do too badly – it was reported in *The Irish Times* that Sonny was even given a state pension for his role in the War of Independence and Civil War. I'd say he got lucky with the people on the pension review panel:

Panellist 1: 'Are there any negatives in his career?'
Panellist 2: 'Well, he shot and killed the greatest Irishman of all time.'
Panellist 1: 'Ah shure, look it, we all have an off day.'

52

FRANK O'CONNOR

Widely regarded as one of the leading short story writers of the twentieth century, Frank O'Connor was referred to as Ireland's Chekhov by W. B. Yeats. (Don't worry if you find this a bit pretentious, I'm getting to the bit on Tanora.)

His story 'Guests of the Nation' was the only good thing about studying English in school. (Unless you are one of those weirdos who enjoyed *King Lear*.) The story is about two British soldiers being held hostage by the IRA during the War of Independence, and it left a lasting impression on anyone who read it. It certainly left a lasting impression on me.

A former IRA man himself, O'Connor moved

to London where he worked for the Ministry of Information and the BBC, before moving again to the States, where he taught in Harvard and Stanford, while writing for *The New Yorker*. Still, he kept writing about his inspiration: the people of Cork.

But none of these achievements are the best thing about Frank O'Connor. The best thing about Frank O'Connor is that he was born Michael O'Donovan. Dropping a typical Cork name and adopting another as a *nom de plume* is the most Cork thing I have ever heard – and I'm not even sure why.

53

ELIZABETH BOWEN

If Elizabeth Bowen had been a man, she would have been recognised as one of the finest novelists of the twentieth century, John Banville once wrote in *The Irish Times*. The prejudice doesn't stop there. If she'd been a Catholic from Dublin, she'd probably have a building named after her in UCD.

But Elizabeth was a member of the Anglo-Irish Ascendancy and her family home, Bowen's Court, was an imposing country house close to Doneraile in North Cork. Both of these things were enough to move her to the fringes of the national consciousness after the War of Independence.

Her book *The Last September* is a gripping eulogy to the former ruling class in North Cork, charting their attempts to continue with their way of life, even as the people who once worked for them arrived in the dead of night to torch their homes.

Bowen is very much of Cork and Ireland, along with other literary giants from that area such as William Trevor. It wasn't all easy living for them in the border regions of North Cork – one wrong turn up there and you could find yourself in Limerick. (Two wrong turns and you could end up in Kerry. Me nerves.)

54

NANO NAGLE

Her story, on the Nano Nagle Place website, opens with, 'If Nano Nagle were alive today, she would be the kind of person to win a Nobel Prize.' (Cork people love a bit of understatement.) In fairness, hers is an impressive story of a woman who defied the anti-Catholic Penal Laws in eighteenth-century Cork to set up seven schools across the city, teaching poor Catholic boys and girls.

What's even more impressive are the museum, cafe and more that opened in 2017 on the grounds of the convent she formed on Douglas Street. Nano Nagle Place is a triumph; the superb food in the Good Day Deli cafe leans towards lentils and Asian influences, and the grounds offer an oasis near the city centre with a Buddhist vibe about them that you'd be hard-stretched to find in Dublin. The Catholic Church has rightly had its critics, but the air of generosity and tranquillity in this historic convent is a fitting tribute to the woman who founded it.

55

MOTHER JONES

Born Mary Harris near Shandon in 1830, you don't tend to hear a lot about this labour rights activist who was once labelled 'the most dangerous woman in America'.

Mary fled Ireland with her family during the famine and moved, through Canada, to the US, where she married ironworker and staunch union man George Jones. An outbreak of yellow fever killed her husband and children, and she lost her house to the Great Chicago Fire of 1871. (I presume she didn't think it was that 'Great').

It was after this that Mary got involved with labour movements, giving speeches to striking miners and railroad workers, who gave her the name 'Mother' back when it was OK to call someone a mother.

She wasn't what you might call the retiring type. Mary was arrested aged eighty-two in West Virginia for her part in a miner's strike, and sentenced to twenty years in prison, although this was followed by a swift pardon from the governor when her supporters did their nut. If you have a granny like that, I want to go to her birthday party.

She died aged ninety-three (though she herself claimed to be one hundred at the time) and was buried in the Miners Cemetery in Mount Olive, Illinois.

As we say in Cork, doubt ya girl.

SECTION 4

THE GREAT OUTDOORS

56

THE BEARA PENINSULA

One of the big attractions of Beara in West Cork is its remoteness. From Dublin. The two million people in Greater Dublin can get to the north of Spain faster than Beara, which is good news for Castletownbere – if not Santander.

Also the roads around Beara aren't great for big coaches, which is fantastic for the independent traveller, unless you enjoy getting stuck behind a bus. The resulting lack of tourist traps is a relief for anyone who doesn't desperately need to buy a woollen leprechaun that was hand-knitted by a four-year-old in Bangladesh. (I'm looking at you the Ring of Kerry, Cliffs of Moher, most of Galway, all of Temple Bar.)

If you're down around Castletownbere don't miss the Dzogchen Beara Buddhist Meditation Centre. There was a laughter therapy session on there when I paid a visit; I could hear them laughing their arses off at nothing at all. Or maybe it was a room full of tourists who had just been told by a deluded jackeen that Dublin is on a par with Barcelona – you can never tell with these things.

The only problem with Beara is that some of it is in Kerry. (This is something I plan to address in my next book: *201 Million Reasons Why Cork is Better than Kerry and I Didn't even Bother to include Hurling*.)

57

FOTA WILDLIFE PARK

Dublin Zoo gets over 1.2 million visitors every year. So now we know how many people like to bring their kids to watch beautiful animals looking really sad.

It's ironic that people who insist on free-range eggs are happy to show their kids an elephant living in a cage. OK, it mightn't be an actual cage, but try and tell that to the elephant.

Unfortunately, it's no consolation to the rhinos that they live next door to Michael D. Higgins. And they're not to know how close they came to getting Peter Casey for a neighbour, a man who'd probably have sent them back to Africa if given half a chance.

Contrast that with Fota Wildlife Park, where you'll find a huge variety of animals rambling around the open spaces, trying to learn a few words of English so they can say, 'Jesus, it's fierce busy above in Dublin, myself and the cubs are haunted that we ended up in Cork.'

However, there is one species of wild animal roaming around Fota that stands out from the rest. These are known as 'The Dubs', weekend breakers who arrive by train and stroll around Fota trying to come to terms with the fact that Cork is clearly much better than Dublin. Go easy on them, that must be tough.

58

CLOSE TO KERRY

I can already hear them below in the Kingdom: 'Yerra, you can keep your auld close to Kerry *plámásing*; we heard what you said about Beara earlier. We're not buying your shagging book anyway.'

Seriously, it's meant as a compliment. Never mind the jokes (Macroom folk are just Kerry people with shoes), Cork people love Kerry, and not just because ye sound like us after a few pints. Face the car west on a sunny Cork morning and you can be down on Inch Strand in a couple of hours. Face the car west on a sunny Dublin morning, but then don't bother starting it because you'll only end up in Athlone.

If surfing or bodyboarding is your thing, you can have half a beach of Atlantic all to yourself in Kerry any time of the year. The nicest thing you can say about the waves around Dublin is that they have erectile dysfunction.

But lookit, as they say across the county bounds, the best thing about Kerry is the people. They are funny, warm and kind of hot, to be honest. They even harbour a charming touch of melancholy, because they are only one county away from perfection.

59

DE VISTAS

Cork city isn't just a centre of excellence for social climbing. It's good for actual climbing as well. Strawberry Hill, Patrick's Hill, Summerhill North and South, Crone's Lane, Nicholas Street, Friar's Walk, Mahony's Avenue and Lover's Walk – they all have a reward at the top, and it's called a view.

You can catch a glimpse of the outer harbour from the top of Churchfield, or get a hint of the Kerry border on a clear day in Shanakiel. It's a reminder that whenever the city gets too much, you're only fifteen minutes away from some wide-open countryside.

There is no such escape in Dublin. Constitution Hill is obviously an ironic name, because it wouldn't even pass for a hill in Holland. And yes, I know there are a couple of hills south of the capital, and people call them the 'Dublin Mountains', because size is everything in a city that wants to be the new London. I hear that a trip to these 'mountains' is very nice, particularly if you enjoy sitting in traffic and waiting for the smog to lift in the hope of getting a glimpse of Dundalk. But let's face it, nothing there can compete with a single view in Cork.

60

DE LOUGH

To an outsider, the Lough is a medium-sized duck pond out towards Togher. But it looms so large in the Cork psyche that most of us are amazed that it isn't visible from space.

We remember being brought there by our parents, and feeling sorry for the birds who migrated there from all over Europe, because they weren't originally from Cork. When our parents explained that these birds could have chosen to winter in Dublin's Bull Island, but came to Cork instead, most of us tried to jump into the Lough so we could give them a hug. ('Ye're a grand load of geese.')

The only downside of the Lough is bumping

into people you know on the way around it. This means a pleasant chat, at first, before you carry on in your opposite directions around the pond. But this means bumping into them again ten minutes later, and starting another chat with them, because chat-refusal is completely un-Cork.

The problem is, it can be exhausting coming up with something new to talk about, which is why you'll often see someone suddenly reversing direction as they go around the Lough. Unfortunately, the other person will often have changed direction for the same reason, and so you'll end up talking to that shagging langer all day. But it doesn't really matter, because you're by the Lough. And sorry Dubs, but Bull Island just doesn't compare.

61
THE COAST

The east coast isn't a complete disappointment. It probably seems amazing to a person from land-locked Laois, or someone who doesn't mind walking halfway to Wales before the water comes up to their knees.

But it's basically a third-rate stretch of coast. Even in their most delusional moments (like when an artist suggested they should light up the Pigeon House Chimneys in Dublin Bay because it would be as beautiful as, wait for it, the Eiffel Tower), no one on the east coast has ever suggested a route called The Wild Irish Sea Way. That's because it would be about as wild as an over-eighties Scottish country dancing night in a convent.

Here's the truth. The shoreline north and south of Dublin is passable if you are from somewhere like Holland – it just about delivers on your low expectations.

But if you are looking for white sand, a proper tide, waves, cliffs and wow-factor, then start in Courtmacsherry and follow the Wild Atlantic Way down west until you reach Dursey Sound. I guarantee you one thing: at no point will you think, what this place needs is two giant chimney stacks belching fumes up into the sky.

62
THE CLIFFS

It's not that Dublin doesn't have a decent cliff walk; it just doesn't have enough of them. The Bray-to-Greystones walk is a perfectly good day out, as long as you don't spend too long in Bray. (Just because it has a promenade doesn't make it right.) Howth Head is OK if you like posh people and expensive seafood. (No wonder we call it the Kinsale of the north.)

The problem is that these two walks have to serve over a million people. This doesn't just mean they're busy; it also means they're a nightmare if you are into Cliff Walk Dating, because you're almost guaranteed to walk into an ex. (Cliff Walk Dating is a great way to show you are the sensitive, outdoors type when you are in fact neither of these things. I can't recommend it highly enough.)

Cork has loads of cliff walks. They are further away from the city distance-wise, but closer time-wise because of traffic. So take your pick from Ballycotton, Nohoval, Courtmacsherry, Seven Heads and even Sheep's Head if you like. Remember to bring someone else, though; otherwise it's not a date. And don't forget, you'd never be able to do this around Dublin without an awkward 'ah shite' moment when you bump into an ex.

63

SCOVING

Definition of 'scoving': to go for a walk, possibly with your old doll.

I've been slow to draw attention to slang in this book, because I think it's one of the few areas where Dublin might have the upper hand. We just can't compete with the way Dublin people use 'yizzers' as a second person plural possessive pronoun. (If you don't know what that means, yizzers English grammar knowledge isn't up to much.)

That said, you can't beat a good scove around Cork. It's a proper walking city, unlike Dublin, which is more a running-for-your-life city because of the way some guy started eyeing up your backpack.

A short scove around the South Parish, south of the south channel of the Lee, doesn't just set a record for the most souths in one sentence. It also takes in the strangely small houses on Crone's Lane, a plaque to a brigade of the Old IRA on a modern-day tattoo parlour, an Aikido martial arts centre and a pint of Beamish out the back of Coughlan's. Best of all, there is a good chance you'll have all of this to yourself. So go on out of that with yizzers Smithfield.

64

WATERSPORTS

No, this isn't the long-awaited section on kinky sexploits. (But there might be one later, so keep on reading.)

This is about a couple heading north on the M8 in a Dublin reg VW camper van with two surfboards on the roof. You can lip-read them saying, 'What the fock were we, like, actually doing, trying to surf in Dublin, when they have waves like that in Cork?' (This is the way posh Dublin people speak; I heard it on Newstalk.)

Cork has an incredible variety of empty beaches all down the coast, so you never know what you might discover. (In contrast, the only thing you're going to discover on a Dublin beach is that not everyone brings their rubbish home.)

It isn't just surfing. There's night kayaking around Baltimore and Lough Hyne, whale watching and more. You might even take a kayak out around the Old Head of Kinsale and jump in for a swim with a giant basking shark. It's hard to imagine a more life-changing experience in Ireland, except maybe that moment in a mediocre Dublin restaurant when you get the bill for two pizzas and a bottle of red: 'Bad news, babes, we're bankrupt.'

65

THE MAD HOUSE

You won't hear Cork people boasting about having the longest building in Ireland. That's because the building in question, Our Lady's Hospital on the Lee Road (aka 'The Mad House', before political correctness made it to Cork), was a mental asylum, and our history of dealing with mental illness is a fair bit south of diabolical. So, basically, pointing out the size of Our Lady's is another way of saying we managed to mistreat more sick people than anyone else in Ireland.

They didn't just lock up people with mental illness. Up to the 1940s, you could have a relative committed simply by telling a court that they were insane, thanks to the Dangerous Lunatics and Dangerous Idiots Acts. (AKA, Come On, We'll Steal the Farm Off Declan.)

Despite its troubled past, the spooky Victorian towers in Our Lady's creates an atmosphere in that part of town, along with an unavoidable reminder that terrible things happen to vulnerable people when the rest of us turn our backs. It's another example of offbeat Cork that you'd struggle to find in prim and proper Dublin.

66

BRIDGE WARS

The conversation is dying so you throw in the 'interesting' fact that you know about O'Connell Bridge. Desperate Irish blokes are devils for trying it on a hot foreigner, only for her to stand up ten seconds later and say, 'You are a bery, bery boring man.' Yet another Spanish woman who doesn't care that O'Connell Bridge is wider than it is long.

Yet, for some reason, Dubliners are bizarrely proud of this, even though it's just another way of saying that the River Liffey is embarrassingly narrow.

Now don't get me wrong, Cork people aren't immune to sharing boring facts likely to repel gorgeous Spaniards. (They remain unimpressed by the fact we have the second largest natural harbour in the world.)

But at least we know better than to boast about our bridges. Most of us have crossed the Brooklyn Bridge at some stage and realise that there is no competing with that kind of thing.

Saying that, though, we also know two things about the Shakey Bridge. It would beat Dublin's Ha'Penny Bridge hands-down in a beauty contest. And Sunday's Well people never talk about crossing it, in case it draws attention to the fact that they live on the northside. (They kept that quiet, didn't they?)

SECTION 5

HISTORY

67

WHAT'S THE MOTTO WITH YOU?

Dublin's motto reads *Obedientia Civium Urbis Felicitas*. Translation: 'We Couldn't Give a Shite to Anything that Happens Outside the M50'. That's obviously not true. For starters, we all know the Latin for M50 is *Jaysus Weptus*.

In fact, the motto means 'Obedient Citizens Make for a Happy City'. Doesn't that make you want to visit Dublin right now, for some fun times? No? Couldn't blame you. It sounds like an ironically cruel sign that you'd see on the gates of a concentration camp.

Dublin's coat of arms? Three castles, with what looks like traffic cones on the turrets. According to the city council's website no one has a clue why the coat of arms has three castles. One theory is it represents what you can buy in Cork for the same price as a roofless garden shed in Dublin 8.

Cork's motto reads *Statio Bene Fide Carinis*. Unlike Dublin's anti-fun motto, this does not mean 'Ye Better Do What Ye're Told, Ye Pack of Langers'. It actually translates as 'A Safe Harbour for Ships'. Take a few moments to savour the basic soundness of Cork's message. Then look at the coat of arms, showing a huge ship sailing into an impossibly narrow gap between two towers. Look even closer and you can see a local guy, saying, 'He's never going to get that in there, Jerry boy.'

68

THE OLD BATTLES

You probably remember the way history was taught in primary school. Battle of Clontarf, good: Ireland beats the tar out of the Vikings, *olé olé olé*. Battle of Kinsale, bad: England beats Ireland, we're stuck with them now.

And then you do a bit of research. (As in, google Battle of Clontarf, take the first one that isn't Wikipedia or the *Daily Mail*, and hope for the best.) It turns out that Clontarf was a battle between the kings of Munster and Leinster, with a few Vikings sprinkled on both sides, because even then it was considered cool to have a few Scandinavians on board. Brian Boru wasn't from Ireland, he was from Munster, which is basically

Cork. So, Cork 1 Dublin 0, on that one.

According to the Internet, which has yet to be wrong, the idea behind the Battle of Kinsale was for the Irish armies to march south from Ulster to Kinsale, hook up with a Spanish army that had landed there, surround the English forces and banish them from the country for good. Unfortunately, the night before the big battle, the Irish got really pissed and failed to hook up with any Spaniards. (It sounds like my stag party.)

Anyway, things went badly wrong, the English won and Ireland didn't become a colony of Spain. If you think the Battle of Kinsale was bad because of this, I'd recommend you google 'Nice conquistadors.'

See? Be careful what you wish for.

69

DE VIKINGS

A 1,000-year-old sword discovered on the site of the old Beamish & Crawford brewery in Cork has changed everything. The sword and the remains of an urban settlement that were also found are thought to pre-date Viking settlements in Waterford – so sorry lads, but our Vikings are older than yours. This confirms what most Leesiders believe – that Cork is better than Waterford in every possible way. And before ye bring up your blaas (a Waterford delicacy), I tried one recently and it's a bread roll.

You might not get to see the old Viking settlement in Cork, because they are building an Event Centre and concert venue on top of it. And in fairness, what's a millennium of local history compared to being able to watch Mumford & Sons in comfort?

But it doesn't take from the fact that Cork is now the oldest Viking city in the country. How do ye like that above in Dublin? And how do ye like the way we haven't tried to cash in on our Vikingness with a splash tour that strips every shred of dignity from everyone who goes on it, followed by an immersive experience thingy hosted by some out-of-work actor in a horny helmet pretending to be from Stockholm? I'd say ye don't like that one bit.

SECTION 6

CULTURE

70

ULYSSES VS THE YOUNG OFFENDERS

I'm reluctant to compare these two. One is an epoch-shaping work of art, celebrated for its experimental language and multi-textured view of a world-famous city. The other is *Ulysses*. In fairness to Joyce, his characters are well drawn, but still nothing on Billy Murphy as played by Shane Casey in *The Young Offenders.*

One of the notable things about *Ulysses* is the famous puzzle that features in it where you have to try getting around Dublin without passing a pub. There are a few ways to tackle this. The first is you could drive around the M50 and head for Cork. That would be my recommendation. (You might pass a pub or two en route, but at least you'll still end up in Cork.)

Alternatively, you could wait eighteen months until the remaining pubs in Dublin are turned into burrito outlets. Or, if waiting isn't your thing, you could just tell the person who set the puzzle that there is a difference between a pub and an enclosed space selling over-priced coddle to sad Japanese people.

Dublin could never produce *The Young Offenders* because capital cities can't laugh at themselves. What would Prague or Barcelona say if they saw Dublin through the lens of a whimsical half-hour comedy with hilarious accents and some ropey acting? And no, I don't mean *Fair City*, although I like where you are going with that one, keep it up.

Just look at the reaction overseas. *Love/Hate*

was eventually shown on Channel 5, the people who dead-horse-flogged *Big Brother* for a few extra years; meanwhile *The Young Offenders* was re-commissioned by the BBC before they even aired the first series. That show is so sound, it gave a role to P.J. Gallagher, who is in fact from Dublin. (OK, they made him play the bad guy, but you can only go so far with these things.)

71

U2 PREFER THE FRANKS

Cork has a soft spot for U2, because they appeared for free at the Lark by the Lee in 1985. (It isn't often we get something for free from Dublin.) The official story on Leeside is that U2 were only there to play support for Cork songster Freddie White, even though they went on after him. You don't hear much about Freddie these days because he didn't ditch his soul to sell records in America.

U2 are the kind of band you can like and admire. But the people who really love them also really love the word 'awesome', and that's a good enough reason to back slowly out of the room.

U2 will never match The Frank and Walters,

because Bono will never write a song that matches the glorious and goofy simplicity of 'After All'. That song captures the essence of Cork and not just because it takes seventeen syllables to get through the letter As in the title.

'After All' comes from a band that will never be invited to Davos. And even if they were, they'd write a song that goes: 'Rich people, ye aren't sound, why won't ye buy us a round?' You see, U2 just don't have that in them.

72

'THE BANKS'

'Molly Malone' and 'The Banks of My Own Lovely Lee' have a lot in common: you don't want to sing either of them until the fourth pint; you don't want to listen to anyone else singing them until the fourteenth; no one knows all the words, and that's actually a good thing.

But if you had to pick one, the choice is between a poor, dead prostitute from Dublin or a beautiful river (with two channels!). So let's hear it for 'The Banks'.

The truth is that Dublin songs are either weird or just plain bullshit, boasting about the Liffey stinking like hell, or about the great people in the Liberties, while at the same time you're trying to force them out so you can build apartment blocks there for hipsters.

Cork has moved on from all that nostalgia. Thanks to cultural highlights like *The Young Offenders* and The Frank and Walters, the go-to song on Leeside these days is the just mentioned 'After All'.

The Frank and Walters hit is unusual – I mean, here you have a Cork man singing about loving something other than Cork. It's also a handy party piece – as everyone will join in with you before the end of 'After all that we've been through' on the second line, which means you can go back to your gin and tonic. Score!

73
FIONA SHAW

Now this is what you call acting aristocracy. Here you have a star of *Harry Potter*, *Fleabag*, *True Blood*, *My Left Foot* and *Killing Eve*, with a richly resonant voice that has made her one of the most sought-after stage actresses in the world. If she was from Dublin, she'd have her own chair on *The Late Late*.

She's actually from Cork, though now living in London. A quick google brings you to an article in *The Sun* titled, 'Who is *Killing Eve* actress Fiona Shaw?', which says that Fiona is from Munster, Ireland. This must be one of the worst examples of fake news on the whole Internet – who in their right mind would want to share their world-class actor with Tipperary?

Even though she's been based in London for a long time, her accent still suggests she never left Cork. This is admirable, given that anyone who doesn't drop their Cork accent in London is sentencing themselves to twenty years of 'You what, mate?'

Shaw is actually a stage name, and she is better known as Fiona Wilson on Leeside, where her father was a highly regarded surgeon in Montenotte. I'd love to make the dig that a professional from Montenotte would be devastated that his daughter only went on to become a world-famous actress. Unfortunately, her parents had a strong interest in the arts, as their home was a venue for poetry readings and music recitals, so they must have been dead proud of their daughter. Just as Cork is.

74

ART GALLERIES

The definition of an intellectual in Cork is someone who goes into the Crawford Art Gallery even when it isn't raining. This isn't a diss on Cork intellectuals. They are very active in the life of the city and it isn't unusual to see both of them inside the Hi-B bar, roaring out twenty reasons why Samuel Beckett isn't a patch on Frank O'Connor.

In fairness, the second city's art galleries can't compete with those in Dublin. But this is actually one of the best things about living in Cork. The lack of world-class galleries here frees up time to do more important things, like feeling smug about ourselves in the English Market, or spray-painting 'Shower of Langers' on the sign for Dublin by the Jack Lynch Tunnel. (We've all been there.)

Meanwhile, the prestigious galleries in Dublin attract two types of people. The first is a scruffy English Lit student from Trinity brandishing a copy of *At Swim-Two-Birds* in the hope of getting the ride from a gullible Yank. The second type is a very sad-looking Chinese couple who can't believe they had to come to Dublin instead of Paris. Who needs that?

75

D'OPERA HOUSE

Cork 1 Dublin 0. That's the score when it comes to having an opera house.

Dublin could always magic up an opera house, I suppose, in the same way that they started selling hummus and kefir in a disused building and said, 'Hey look, goys, now we have a market like that one in Cork.'

The reason it won't work, though, is heritage. Cork has always been a big fan of opera. Why? Italians. During the nineteenth and early twentieth centuries, the big Italian opera stars would stop off at Cobh on their way to the States. Once ashore, they'd get the train up to Cork, where they'd be greeted by huge crowds eager to see musical stars. It was like in the 1980s, when Cork would go bananas for Michael Jackson and Stockton's Wing.

These Italian opera stars would play the Opera House, the stalls packed with people from all walks of Cork life, singing along with the arias. Listen closely the next time you're in there for an echo of, 'Who are you to come here over from It-lee and tell me I can't blast out ten minutes of Rigoletto?'

The tradition continues today. Cara O'Sullivan is a world-famous soprano. Cork native John O'Brien has a name for ground-breaking opera productions in the Opera House, The Everyman and further afield. You just won't get that in Dublin.

76

THEATRE

We rejoin our unfortunate friends, the disappointed Japanese tourists, as they head out for an evening of culture in Dublin. They are in the home town of some of the greatest playwrights in the modern world, so hopes are extremely high. Unfortunately, so are a lot of the people they pass on the streets of Dublin, as our quiet Japanese friends stroll around looking for a decent play.

It's not the easiest search in the world, given the choice is between Disney on Ice or a play about a fella who lives with his controlling mother on a fictional Aran Island. It isn't all negative, however. Our Japanese friends are hugely impressed with the way the Dublin audience manages to neck three gin and tonics during the interval, and wish they could have done so themselves, to help them get through another hour of a fella and his controlling mother on a fictional Aran Island.

Cork has no such pretensions. It's all about the fun. The Everyman and the Opera House would probably put on four pantos a year if they could get away with it. And they probably would get away with it too, because if there is one thing Cork audiences love, it's a man in a dress.

77

NIGHTCLUBS

I've had a thing against Dublin nightclubs since the age of eight, when I was travelling down Baggot Street by bus and spotted Zhivago. Always a fan of their slogan, which appeared in a cinema advert at the time, I shouted, 'Dad look, it's that nightclub Zhivago, where love stories begin', and every last person on the bus started laughing at me and my Cork accent. Anyway, thanks for letting me share.

My next experience of Dublin nightclubs was in my mid-twenties, drinking wine in Leggs on Leeson Street. Why they didn't call that club Leggless still bothers me today. Why they used the term 'wine' for the drink they served was another cause for concern. Whatever it was, the hangover has lasted for twenty-seven years and counting.

Meanwhile, in Cork, they had Sir Henry's. Nirvana played there in August 1991, about eight seconds before they became world-famous. And then there was Sweat Night, a regular event that started in 1988 and put Cork on the map for house music fans across Europe. By the time dance music and raves arrived in Dublin, it was already a bit naff down in Cork.

Sorry if I seem dismissive of your nightclub scene, Dublin. I'm sure you had one or two passable clubs down the years, but I don't want to hear about them because yiz all laughed at me once on a bus.

78

CRYSTAL SWING

In a way, we were probably too close to Crystal Swing, at first. We saw Derek singing cheesy love songs to his sister and thought, that's a bit much, even for people from East Cork. It didn't sit right, just like Derek's jacket.

They viewed it differently in Los Angeles. (They view a lot of things differently in Los Angeles, says you.) Ellen DeGeneres watched their video, said, 'If loving Crystal Swing is wrong, I don't want to be right', and invited them on her show. Five seconds into their video for 'He Drinks Tequila', though, you could see where Ellen was coming from.

The beauty of Crystal Swing is that they're

in on their own joke. While you are fussing over the death of taste and western civilisation, they are hamming their way through one of the worst music videos of all time. (We're talking T'Pau levels here. If you haven't heard of them, lucky you.)

So thank you, Ellen, for giving us a dose of perspective. We'd been led to believe that the only authentic Irish act was a singer-songwriter telling us why he can't bring himself to talk to a girl on the bus. If you think there isn't room on the Irish playlist for tons of cheese, then the Crystal Swing joke is on you.

79

'THE BOYS OF FAIRHILL'

The original 'The Boys of Fairhill' is an ode to old-school Cork pastimes like drag hunting, bowling and drinking stout that isn't from Dublin. You'll find a video of Jimmy Crowley and Stoker's Lodge singing it on YouTube, interspersed with a surreal chat by some harriers drinking stout not from Dublin and saying how much they love their hounds, not to mention their wives. (I very nearly gave that video its own section in this book.)

The genius of the song is the way it can take on new verses. The lines people know now – 'The smell from Patrick's Bridge is wicked, how does Father Mathew stick it', or 'Blackpool girls are very rude, they go swimming in the nude', or 'Blackpool boys are very nice, I have tried them once or twice' – seem to have been added later, possibly by Dublin people trying to wreck the song with vulgarity. I'm only half messing here, by the way – The Wolfe Tones' version isn't the kind of thing you could sing in front of a priest. (Although that might depend on the priest.)

All that remains now is to say that I think it's time for a new verse: 'The Dubs they are a pack of shams, boasting that they have two trams, here's up them all, says the boys of Fairhill'.

80

SMINKY SHORTS

Give Up Yer Aul Sins is funny enough, if you have been at the gin and tonic. A young girl explaining the Bible in a Dublin accent will always get a laugh, and not just because the Bible is hilarious in an 'imagine we used to believe that' sort of way.

But *Sminky Shorts* cartoons are different. Nobody knows why they are funny. There is nothing inherently hilarious about a bird auditioning to say cock-a-doodle-doo. But when you watch what the creator of *Sminky Shorts* (and the superb *Martin's Life*), Andrew James, does with it, you will be deep into coughing-up-a-lung territory. The sketch where the horse stands by a puddle and says 'I can't do it' should probably come with a health warning. It's not unusual to wake up in the middle of the night and reflect that the *Sminky Short* 'Tommy is stone mad for speed' is, in fact, the pinnacle of all human creation.

In the end, it's best not to analyse this too much. We should just accept that there is something hilarious about a bunch of animals with a mid-Cork accent. (Or Macroom people, as they are known in the city.)

81

CORCADORCA

What do Cillian Murphy and Eileen Walsh have in common?

They both starred in the play *Disco Pigs*, written by Enda Walsh (who is actually from Dublin, but we'll overlook that for now). Walsh was in exile in Cork in the mid 1990s, when Corcadorca Theatre Company founder Pat Kiernan asked him to write something. The result was *Disco Pigs*, an intense play involving two actors and two chairs that ended up touring the world.

While the actors and writer went on to the West End and Hollywood, Kiernan and Corcadorca stayed in Cork, making what public house theatre critics might describe as 'weird shit'.

This is because Corcadorca productions are site-specific pieces, performed outside a theatre, so our public house critics can't slink downstairs and down three gin and tonics during the intermission.

In fairness to these critics, you'd need a shot of liquid refreshment to stick with a lot of conventional plays. But with Corcadorca, you just immerse yourself and go along for the ride. As weird shit goes, it's one of the best things about theatre in Ireland. And just in case you've forgotten, it's based in Cork. (The Dublin crowd wouldn't know what to make of it.)

82

DE BUTTERA AND DE BARRACKA

They're the kind of brass bands you just won't get in Dublin. The Barracka is The Barrack Street Band, founded in 1837 by Father Mathew as a temperance band. If you don't know what temperance means, I'm not surprised, because it means abstaining from alcohol, so the word comes with a trigger warning for generations of Irish people. (That was when the pub was considered a safe space.)

The Buttera is the Butter Exchange Band, founded in 1878 to give the northsiders something to march to. They seemed to have had a more liberal attitude to gargle than their southside rivals. According to the Buttera website, the committee decreed in 1931 that they should bring three gallons of beer when they went on an outing. (And that was probably just for Mossie.) Anyone who didn't drink got two packets of fags. Now that's what I call a recruitment drive.

The two bands come into their own at the Patrick's Day parade. In fairness, the Paddy's Day parade in Cork can't compete with the one in Dublin. In principle, I've nothing against watching kids from a local judo club ambling past waving at their mams, but it can be very cold at that time of the year. At least, that is, until the Buttera and the Barracka swing into view and warm you up, partially with laughter at the thought of a brass band trying to get people to stop drinking on Patrick's Day.

83

'THE BOLD THADY QUILL'

The bold in the title of this famous song is pronounced 'bould'. (We like to mispronounce things in Cark, as it's known by half the locals.)

Thady Quill was a poor labourer who did none of the things attributed to him in the song. He was engaged as a labourer by Johnny Tom Gleeson in North Cork around 1892. Johnny Tom fancied himself as a balladeer, and rather than paying Thady actual cash, he offered to immortalise him in song. You wouldn't get away with that kind of employee exploitation these days, unless you manufacture smartphones in China. However, Thady was delighted with this deal, which probably explains why he failed to attract a woman and died a bachelor.

So there you have it. It turns out Thady wasn't actually your man 'for ramblin', for rovin', for football and sportin', for drinking black porter as fast as you fill'. But who cares? As Homer Simpson said of a movie where a man gets hit in the nads by an American football, 'The Bold Thady Quill' works at every level.

84

STAYING' LIVE

It would be wrong to say Dublin doesn't have a live music scene. Everyone knows there's a production line near Swords where they turn out squeeze-box players to satisfy the demands of Temple Bar. And they must never stop looking for the next U2, for reasons that aren't immediately clear.

But Cork has a string of small venues where people who love playing play to people who love listening. I doubt anyone is getting rich at the trad sessions in Sin É, An Spailpín Fánach or The Franciscan Well. That said, I doubt anyone is getting bored in those venues or in places like the Corner House, Coughlan's, Cyprus Avenue, Crane Lane or in Live at St Luke's.

As you'd expect from the city that nurtured Rory Gallagher, Jimmy Crowley and the Sultans of Ping, there's no shortage of choice. One night and one pub sums up the scene on Leeside – Monday night in Charlie's on Union Quay, with Hank Wedel and Ray Barron. They've operated an open-house policy for this residency since 1994, where musicians from all over the world can rock up and join in. My friend Con tells me it's the berries.

SECTION 7

SPORT

85

THE OLYMPICS

It's wrong to say that Dubliners have no sense of humour. Every now and again one of them suggests that Dublin is ready to host the Olympics, and everyone breaks the world record for laughter.

Achtung Dubliners: the Olympic authorities have been on to say you'll need more than two tramlines, even if they do intersect. And you'd fall well short in terms of bed capacity for the large army of doctors attached to national teams, there to administer entirely legal over-the-counter medicines to the athletes in a transparent manner, it says here.

Cork has no Olympic notions, although the Marina would be amazing for the rowing. Where

Cork excels in terms of the Olympics is in actually winning medals. Dr Pat O'Callaghan won back-to-back gold medals for the hammer back in the day. Sonia O'Sullivan and Rob Heffernan brought home medals in more recent years, while the O'Donovan brothers have turned Skibbereen into the rowing capital of the world. Better still, as I mentioned earlier, they made an appearance on *The Graham Norton Show*, proving beyond any doubt that there is more than one accent in Cork. (Not to mention language.)

86
MUNSTER

You can't question the fervour and commitment of Munster rugby fans (when they're winning). It's so strong that Cork people are willing to travel to Limerick. Not only that, they have been known to hug the Limerick person sitting next to them in Thomond Park following a try. If that home game happens to be against an Italian team, a Cork person could be looking at seven hugs with a Limerick person. Like I say, commitment.

Well that, and a shared hatred for 'goys' called Oisin from Booterstown who can be heard honking about Leinster from four pubs away. There is so much to dislike there. (Starting with the brown shoes. Seriously, Oisin, don't go around calling people boggers when you're dressed like the backing singer at a Nathan Carter gig.)

Oddly enough, the Munster bond isn't entirely built on a hatred for Oisin and his friends (also called Oisin). The real problem here is Galway. Limerick and Cork people hate Galway. We hate the way it was adopted by Oisin and his friends in the 1990s as a smaller Dublin on the west coast. All that plucky Connacht bullshit is a Dublin thing. The truth is that Munster people die a little inside when Connacht looks like a proper rugby team. In our darker moments, we love it when Galway gets put in its place. (So much so that we give each other a little hug.)

87

WOMEN'S GAA

As I write, the Cork Ladies footballers have eleven All-Ireland titles to Dublin's three. Enough said there. As for camogie, it's Cork twenty-eight to Dublin's twenty-six, with Cork taking four of the last five O'Duffy Cups.

It seems unlikely the Dubs will catch up any time soon, given that they haven't won a title since 1984. Mind you, this is the GAA, so you can't rule out a €4 squillion grant to fast-track camogie in the capital, seeing as it would be a shame if Dublin didn't win every year. If they can do it for men's football, they should do the same for camogie. Otherwise, it's sexism, innit?

Whatever happens, it's safe to say that

camogie is on the rise, with Cork players like Briege Corkery, Rena Buckley and Ashling Thompson approaching superstar status. It helps explain why crowds of over 20,000 are the norm in Croke Park on All-Ireland final day. Who knows, the GAA might even go crazy and use the shiny new Páirc Uí Chaoimh for a camogie decider one of these days. This is assuming Cork doesn't make the final, of course, because it would be grossly unfair to give one team home advantage for a big game. Isn't that right Dublin?

88

MEN'S GAA

I won't waste too much time on hurling. At the time of writing, Cork has thirty senior All-Irelands, whereas Dublin has six. It doesn't look like spending a fortune will help the Dubs here.

Which is more than you can say for the men's football. Dublin gets enough development funding from the GAA to buy every one of their players a big gold house. Unfortunately, they don't do that, and pump all their money into training facilities instead, so they can choose between thirty-three man-machines to go out and humiliate Westmeath. (You could be looking at the end of the Leinster Championship if the authorities broaden their ban on blood sports.)

And yet they somehow manage to only have twenty-eight titles to Cork's eight. This is despite the fact that Cork footballers are mainly drawn from two families in Skibbereen; their own mams wouldn't go to see them play if the Cork hurlers were on TV; and a recent Cork team had to make their own gym in Fermoy. Worse still, they usually have to play Kerry, where people grow up with nothing else to do outside of football and tax dodging. It's a miracle Cork footballers ever win a thing.

89

ROB HEFFERNAN

Super-smug because you and your partner go for a jog together on a Sunday morning, as long as it's dry? Well, Rob and his wife, Marian, were the first Irish couple to compete in the same Olympic Games.

Rob is also the first Irishman to compete in five Olympic Games, winning a delayed bronze medal for the 50k walk in the 2012 London Olympics, when it emerged that the Russian guy who won gold might have added something to his cornflakes. (They were slow to suspect him, at first, because Russian sport has such a good reputation for being clean.)

Speaking of Russia, Rob went to Moscow

the following year and won gold at the World Championships. He won these medals race-walking, which can look a bit like a person with diarrhoea making a bolt for the jacks. It takes restraint and grit, and a fair amount of 'I couldn't give a shit what I look like on television'.

It will be some time before an Irish athlete matches Rob's achievements. The thing about race-walking is that you're not allowed to run – this will never suit anyone from Dublin because they're always in such a rush. (Did I mention that Dublin is fierce busy?)

90

PUNDITS

Wanted for sports punditry work: an unpredictable, cranky, argumentative individual who could start a fight in solitary confinement.

That's actually the recipe for a Cork person. Or two Cork people in particular: George Hook and Roy Keane. You are not allowed to talk about George in public these days, as he's been scrubbed from history after making some very ill-considered and hurtful comments. But long before 'trucking it up over the gain line' became the kind of thing you could say to another person in actual conversation, George was helping us to fall in love with rugby. Or at least fall in love with George comparing the first half to some ancient

Greek battle, just to see if he could make Conor O'Shea cry.

Roy Keane's main message these days, when he isn't taunting Arsenal fans, is to suggest life would be much better for Man Utd if it was still him and Scholesy playing in midfield. This is catnip for any men over forty, trying to get to grips with the fact that it's no longer 1999.

Team Cork Pundits has no shortage of talent coming through either. It's hard to look away when Donal Óg Cusack or Ronan O'Gara are dissecting hurling or rugby on the telly. And former camogie star Anna Geary has mastered the art of sticking the knife in while wearing her butter-wouldn't-melt smile. That's punditry gold right there.

91

THE RCYC

The Royal Cork Yacht Club is the oldest yacht club in the world. (Their motto is 'Looking down on people since 1720'.) More importantly, it's the oldest yacht club in Ireland, so in your face nouveau riche sailor boys above in Dublin.

The high point of the social season on Leeside is Cork Week in the RCYC. This is where the great and the good gather and try to figure out everyone else's net worth by the quality of their tan.

It's almost impossible to find someone there who didn't go to a fee-paying school such as Presentation Brothers, Christians or Scoil Mhuire. (There's a quick way to find out if someone went to one of these schools – wait ten seconds and they'll tell you.)

Unlike Dublin snobs, who openly wish they were Jacob Rees-Mogg, Cork snobs have to hide their privilege, because you don't want a name for being 'up yourself'. So don't be alarmed if an RCYC type throws a 'like' or 'boy' into a sentence – he's just pretending to be the same as someone who doesn't have three bank accounts in the Cayman Islands.

92

ROAD BOWLING

Nobody calls it that, of course. It is simply known as 'bowling', with the bow pronounced as in 'take a bow', particularly by RCYC types who want to feel like they are down with their gardener.

The game is between two bowlers, trying to toss a twenty-eight-ounce metal ball along a country road in as few throws as possible. So yes, it's basically golf without the shit jumpers.

The world champion often comes from Cork, and not just because the only other bowling hotspots are Armagh and parts of Germany where there is nothing else to do. A lot of gambling money changes hands at these events, and the phones would be ringing off the hook in the

Revenue Commissioners the next day, with fellas ringing in to declare their winnings, says no one.

There is something uniquely Cork about driving down narrow roads between high ditches on a summer's evening and happening upon a bunch of cars parked tight into the side of the road.

With a bit of luck you'll get to see someone lofting a bowl: it's elegant and powerful, rather than just a show of brute strength. It won't be long before you're allowed on your way, more often than not waved through by an officious little man called Mossie in a high-viz jacket. Unless, of course, you're in a Dublin reg car, in which case you'll be held back for a while. Mossie doesn't like people from Dublin.

93

IRELAND'S FITTEST FAMILY

AKA, Where Retired Cork Sports Stars Launch Their TV Careers (plus Davy Fitz). You can see why they went with the first name for the TV show – #WRCSSLTTCPDF would use up most of your characters in a tweet.

Donncha O'Callaghan, Anna Geary and Derval O'Rourke are three of the four coaches on the hit RTÉ show. Davy Fitzgerald is the other one, and he's an honorary Cork man at this stage, having been deemed to reach the required levels of grudge-fuelled rage.

The Cork coaches have a number of advantages over any Dublin rivals, what with being funny and good-looking. Anna Geary was born for TV, Derval O'Rourke is funny-sarcastic (we love that) and Donncha O'Callaghan is incredibly likeable, even though we know he doesn't drink. (Irish people find it hard to trust a non-drinker.)

Of course by the time you read this, the Cork coaches might have been replaced by ones from Dublin. It would be easy to put this down to a typical bias against Cork people in the capital, so I will. (We all will. Half of Cork will be on to Neil Prendeville on RedFM to complain; the other half will be on to P.J. Coogan on Cork's 96FM.)

SECTION 8

FOOD AND DRINK

94

BARRY'S TEA

The few people in Cork that drink Lyons tea probably regard themselves as mavericks. Trust me, that's not what everyone else in Cork calls them. (There is a word way beyond 'langer' for just that kind of carry-on.)

It's unfair to do down Lyons, just because it is no longer made in Ireland. It's not as if Barry's Tea comes from the verdant tea plantations of Carrigaline, after all. But this is a book about Cork being better than Dublin, so go away out of that with yeer Lyons.

Also, Barry's wins hands down when it comes to TV ads. The standout one is where the girl and the guy who have known each other 'forever' end up working in the same office, and he asks her out and she says, 'Is this a date?' and it is really.

It's both touching and yet odd, for two reasons. First of all, he's a guy under the age of a hundred who drinks tea at work and she still doesn't think he's a weirdo. Secondly, it was 2008, so they had to get together without using Tinder. I mean, that's just disgusting.

95

DELICIOUS, MAN

At some point in the past forty years, Cork must have put up signs across Europe saying, 'Wanted: 40,000 Hippies'. It's fair to say that they all came and influenced the way we live here. Let's just say that loads of Cork people spent their college years in a bedsit on Magazine Road discussing Toffee Pops with a psychology student from Skibbereen called Moonhoney. Actually, it was just an afternoon, but it seemed way longer.

This hippy hinterland around Cork was fertile ground for a mix of traditional and exotic food start-ups. (The munchies are a great motivator.) The result is a range of world-class food producers (not all hippies) doing amazing things with smoked fish, cheese, poultry, meat, vegetables, olives and more. (Before listing a few, I'd like to make it clear that none of the following foodies ever smoked cannabis and if they ever met Moonhoney, she can't remember it.)

A stroll through the English Market reveals Frank Hederman's Smoked Salmon, Tom Durcan's Spiced Beef, Declan O'Flynn's take on the modern sausage, Kay Harte's Farmgate restaurant and much more. There's also a whole aisle dedicated to fish. You just can't get that in Dublin.

96

TRADITIONAL DISHES

Not all Cork food is great. It's hard to make a case for food culture in a city where people are openly cooking bodice for their family. In case you haven't heard the term before, bodice is the Cork word for revenge. You serve it to someone who clearly did you some terrible injustice in the past. The recipe is 'take perfectly good spare ribs and boil the shite out of them instead of putting them in the oven'. It's like somebody in Cork misread the instructions 200 years ago and their descendants have been too embarrassed to admit their mistake. They are also terrified to call over to their mam's house, in case she is cooking bodice. The smell. Jesus.

And yet it's better than coddle, Dublin's so-called claim to culinary fame. Coddle is shorthand for 'Yiz are going to regret this.' The recipe is to find some scraps in the bin, spit on them, add two sprigs of parsley and stir for ten minutes while saying, 'Yiz thinks yiz are great with your Asian fusion doughnuts and dat.' Delicious.

And before you jump in with 'What about Dublin Bay Prawns?', well I've seen Dublin Bay up close and I wouldn't eat something taken out of there if my life depended on it.

97

PARADISO

Or Cafe Paradiso to anyone over the age of twenty-five. The vegetarian restaurant on the Western Road is the place to bring anyone who normally makes a frowny face because they can't get a steak. It could convert the most passionate meat-eater into a vegetarian in two hours flat.

Denis Cotter co-founded it in 1993, back when the veggie scene in Dublin was still in its dreadlocks and lentils phase. A good name for a veggie restaurant in the capital then would have been: Just Eat Your Fucking Nut Roast, OK?

Meanwhile, Cotter was doing amazing things with aubergine, artichoke and stinky cheese. Better still, he was sourcing his ingredients from small growers that he knew in the local area. Cafe Paradiso had a heart long before the rest of the world cottoned on to air miles and those imposters who claim that everything they offer is 'made with passion in small batches by local artisan suppliers'. (AKA, my dad gave me twenty grand so I started baking gluten-free cookies as a kind of a business, for the craic, like.)

The service is the other thing that sets Paradiso apart. A lot of visitors from Dublin are shocked to find staff that actually smile at you, rather than acting like they just got some terrible news about some flesh-eating disease.

98

TAKE IT AWAY

You probably can't afford to eat in Paradiso every day, of course (unless you can, in which case have you seen my GoFundMe page?). For takeaway at Cork prices, head up Barrack Street to the Bandon Road, where you'll find Jackie Lennox's chip shop, the best on the planet (along with KCs in Douglas), and home to the finest lip-readers in the world.

Order Taker: 'Who's next?'

Completely Pissed Punter, fifteen metres away, in a queue stretching out the door, with a bus passing just behind him: 'Hona-wona, wona-hona, wona-hona-hona-wona, no onions on the second, wona, wona-hona.'

Order Taker: 'Two Jackies, no onions on one, cheese and onion pie. Who's next?'

Genius. Now head north-east down Barrack Street. Artisan pizza to the right (La Tana), artisan pizza with pint to the left (Tom Barry's). You'd get it in Dublin, but not at this price. Turn right at the bottom of the hill. Miyazaki takeaway. You can't get this in Dublin, not at any price. Sidle up behind the Dublin hipsters in the queue who have travelled down to Cork because they read the latest Miyazaki review in *The Irish Times*. Whisper the average price of a house around here, compared to what they paid in Stoneybatter. Try not to laugh when they start crying; it's just not a great look.

99

STOUT CORK

Beamish, Murphy's and Guinness. That's 2–1 Cork right there.

It's a miracle that Beamish is still with us. There was a time when its sole fan was a guy called Donie on Evergreen Street and he was only drinking it out of spite. But Beamish has found its feet among city drinkers again, wherever hipsters gather to talk about their beards.

I started drinking Murphy's in my early twenties in Cork because I thought it marked me out as an intellectual. I also liked the smoky flavour and the way you could drink loads of it without hiccuping your tonsils over the bar. Then a terrible thing happened. I moved to the capital, where only a few pubs served proper Cork stout, and the keg had been sitting there for so long it had developed a Dublin accent. They also had only one Murphy's glass in the pub and you sensed you were probably sharing it with a guy from Mallow with a runny nose. So I did what Cork people are always forced to do in Dublin: I developed a taste for Guinness.

After fourteen years of Dublin and its treacherous stout, I moved back to Cork, where I now drink Beamish in a pub that doesn't serve Guinness. Not that I'd be looking for it, anyway.

100

CRAFTY CORK

Speaking of hipsters and beer, a 2017 report by Bord Bia found that Cork has ten microbreweries against Dublin's seven. (It's all about small wins when you come from the second city.)

You might say this is nothing to crow about. Craft beer seems like a good idea, until you wake up the next day with a pale-ale headache the size of Macroom.

Worse again, some craft beers feel like they are made by people who googled 'how to make beer in the bath', followed by 'bullshit provenance story involving a hairy Gael, Vikings or an ancient well'.

But when craft beer is good, it's great. It's

certainly better than big brand lagers – one sip there and you're wondering why they didn't call it Wrestler's Jockstrap. (It didn't play well in the focus groups, apparently.)

If you want world-beating craft beer in Ireland now, you're talking about places like Franciscan Well, Rising Sons, 8 Degrees and Elbow Lane. Three of those are in Cork city centre, with 8 Degrees in Mitchelstown. No wonder Cork is chokka with hipster types cycling around town showing off their beards. (And that's just the women, says you, full of hipster hate.)

101

TANORA

You didn't seriously think I was going to do a book about Cork and not include the fizzy drink Tanora as one of the 101 reasons why it's better than Dublin? You might as well write a book about Germany and skip the twentieth century.

Tanora does enough to earn its place in the book with the classic advertising ditty, 'Wet your whistle with Tanora, it's the wan you'll want some-more-aah.' That's ditty gold right there, presumably from the pen of the Cork Hibernians fan who came up with 'Starry Starry Night, Paint your Langer Green and White'.

Fizzy drinks are out of fashion these days, because we've all seen Channel 5 shows with names like I Drank 76 bottles of Coke and Look at Me Now. But that doesn't prevent us Cork people from force-feeding Tanora to our kids in a fit of nostalgia.

'Put down your new shagging iPhone and have a slug of this,' we shout at them over Christmas dinner, pretending that things were better in the past. At this point their little faces light up, possibly because of sugar poisoning, as they realise that Tanora is deliciously bold and cranky and different, a bit like the city it comes from.

They pause for a second and say:

'Why does this taste so good, Dad?'

'Because it isn't from Dublin.'

You might as well start them young.

ACKNOWLEDGEMENTS

A big shout out to my wife, Rose, and kids, Joe and Freda. The fact that you three live in Cork is one of the best things about the city as far as I'm concerned. A special mention too for my mother, Aileen. Like any good Cork mother, she brought me up to believe that I'm from the best place on the planet. Finally, a word for the good people at Mercier, Patrick, Noel and Wendy, who reined me in a bit when I was inclined to go over the top.